ACE YOUR TEACHER INTERVIEW

149 Fantastic Answers to Tough Interview Questions

Anthony D. Fredericks, Ed.D.

jist Works
America's Career Publisher®

Ace Your Teacher Interview: 149 Fantastic Answers to Tough Interview Questions

© 2012 by Anthony D. Fredericks

Published by JIST Works, an imprint of JIST Publishing
875 Montreal Way
St. Paul, MN 55102
Phone: 800-648-JIST   E-mail: info@jist.com   Website: www.jist.com

Acquisitions Editor: Lori Cates Hand
Development Editor: Grant E. Mabie
Production Editors: Heather Stith, Jeanne Clark
Cover Designer: Honeymoon Image & Design Inc. and Aleata Halbig
Interior Designer and Layout: Aleata Halbig
Proofreader: Laura Bowman
Indexer: Cheryl Ann Lenser

Printed in the United States of America

17 16 15 14 13 12   9 8 7 6 5 4 3 2 1

Library of Congress Cataloging-in-Publication data is on file with the Library of Congress.

ISBN 978-1-59357-866-4

Dedication

To _____ :

(write your name here)

A prospective teacher—one who will have a significant impact on the lives of students and the future of education!

Table of Contents

Part II: During the Interview

Part III: After the Interview

Acknowledgments

This book benefitted enormously from the contributions, deliberations, suggestions, and input of numerous individuals. Their professional assistance made this a far better resource and a more engaging tome than I could have written on my own. I am eternally grateful to old friends and newfound acquaintances for their advice and direction, counsel, and wisdom.

First, my students at York College of Pennsylvania deserve a thunderous standing ovation and a plethora of "high fives." They have suffered and endured, shared and suggested—with heaping measures of good humor and positive dedication. That the teaching profession will be enhanced by their service is a given; that this book has been strengthened by their ideas and perspectives is equally significant. They are the *crème de la crème* of educators, and it is my honor and pleasure to work with them every day and every semester.

To all the principals and administrators who invited me into their offices and their schools over the years, I extend a warm and gracious "Thank you." I was privileged and honored to communicate with an eclectic array of sincere, committed, and insightful individuals from a wide range of educational institutions throughout the United States and Canada. Each provided me with invaluable tips, successful procedures, and practical insights; they allowed me to pick their brains (often when they least expected it) and view the realities and dynamics of well-executed, thoughtful interviews.

I also extend a warm appreciation to all the reviewers of this book—those friends and colleagues who took valuable time out of hectic schedules to assess the utility of this resource and its practicality for tomorrow's teachers. Enormous cheers and grateful hugs go to Nancy Sinkus (Slatington, PA), Susan Fetner (Morganton, NC), George Severns (Dover, PA), Anita Meinbach (Miami, FL), K. C. Cassell (Orme, AZ), Jan Kristo (Orono, ME), Lynn Boyleston (Lexington, SC), and Cathy Gaarden (Rio Rancho, NM).

I am eternally thankful to Lori Cates Hand, who, although she is no longer with the company, took on this project for JIST Publications with enormous enthusiasm and unmitigated support. She was an early advocate of the ideas and message within these pages, and her fingerprints are liberally sprinkled throughout the chapters.

This book would have been considerably less than it is without the expert editorial guidance, keen eye, and professional attention to detail of its developmental editor—Grant Mabie. Grant is one of those rare editors keenly aware of how to work with an author to maintain a voice, shape a manuscript, and design a product—all with a remarkable *joie de vivre* that is both engaging and inspiring. Most important, Grant is the consummate professional—genuine, devoted, and personable. What a joy!

Above all, I want to acknowledge you—the reader. You are about to embark on an incredibly rewarding and exciting career. You have spent considerable time and devoted substantial energy to get to this stage in your professional development, and I want to salute those efforts, applaud your determination, and celebrate your possibilities. Thank you for all your contributions to education—those that have gotten you to this point, and those that will ensure your teaching success in the future.

—Anthony D. Fredericks, Ed.D.

INTRODUCTION

L et's begin this book with a basic fact of life:

> The person who gets the job is not necessarily the best qualified candidate.
> It's the person who knows how to best nail the interview! In the end, employ-
> ers want to hire individuals they feel will be a good "fit" for the job and for the
> organization. They hire people they like both personally and professionally.[*]

Does that statement scare you? Does it worry you? Does it make you question all
those methods courses you took, all those papers you wrote, all those exams you
sweated over, and all those late-night sessions you spent writing behavioral objectives, anticipatory sets, and assessment protocols during your student teaching experience? I hope not! The statement above should give you a perspective, as well as a
challenge, on the task before you—*acing your teacher interview!*

Here's another fact of life: You can send out all the resumes, contact all the school
districts in your state, and write all the cover letters you want—but you can't get
a teaching position unless you interview. Without the interview, there can be no
teaching. Do well on the interview, and the job is yours! Do poorly on the interview, and—no matter how impressive your credentials may be, no matter how high
your GPA is, no matter how many textbooks you have read, no matter how stellar
your letters of recommendation may be, no matter how much time you've spent
around kids—the simple truth is you'll never get the position! Simply put:

> The teacher interview will make you or break you!

When I was in college (and long before I met my wife), my roommate set me up
with a blind date. We went to dinner and a movie. It soon became apparent that

---

[*] Caryl Krannich and Ron Krannich, *Nail the Job Interview! 101 Dynamite Answers to
Interview Questions*, 6th ed. (Manassas Park, VA: Impact Publications, 2007).

we had absolutely nothing in common. She was from Texas; I was from California. I grew up surfing; she grew up quilting. I was a long-distance runner; she hated sports. I loved Mexican food; she was into steak and potatoes. I enjoyed action movies; she preferred romances. I was a liberal; she was a conservative. Conversation was stilted, uncomfortable, and strained. I had her back at her dorm by 9:30 (imagine!). It was very obvious there would be no second date.

Interviews are like first dates. You are trying to get to know someone. You're trying to enjoy each other's company. You want to know if this will be a long-term relationship or just a one-night stand. You want to learn as much about each other as you can in the short time available. Your decision to continue the relationship is often based on the "chemistry" that takes place during the initial encounter. A first date and an interview are, quite simply, opportunities to exchange information about each other. Each person wants to know if this is a "match" or if this is a "miss."

As Caryl and Ron Krannich once said, "Interviews don't just count—they count the most." An interview is your one opportunity to demonstrate what you know and who you are. That information is not always apparent from the applications, resumes, and letters of recommendation you submit to a school. That information is, however, the crux of a good interview. Successful interviews are all about knowledge and performance: how you present yourself, your responses to questions, and the match between your philosophy and that of the school. Remember, first and foremost, that a school wants to hire a person…a personality…a teacher; the school does not want a resume…an application…or a grade point average.

Keep in mind that a principal or teacher-selection committee is looking for two outstanding qualities in any teacher candidate:

1) Will this individual fit in with our school or district philosophy/educational climate, and

2) Will this individual contribute significantly and positively to the education of the students in his or her charge?

There is, of course, another question you must also answer—one that is never asked, but one you must always address. That one question is so important it has been given its own chapter (Chapter 6). It is, as you might expect, a question you should practice answering several times in advance of any interview.

This book includes information on how to prepare for a forthcoming interview, how to showcase your individual strengths throughout an interview, and what to do immediately after an interview is concluded. I've included information on the 149 most commonly asked questions in teacher interviews (and the answers that most impress interviewers), what to do with tricky questions, how to handle situational scenarios, and the kinds of questions that you should be posing, too. I also share some strategies that will reduce your stress for a first interview and get you ready for a second or third round of interviews.

There are also several bonus features sprinkled throughout this book. These include

- **Insider Tips:** These sections include valuable information from professional interviewers (both in education and in business) and from other teachers who have been through a few interviews themselves. You'll get insider information available in no other resource.

- ✔**Extra Credit:** These are tips that can make the difference between a good interview and a great interview. The emphasis here is on practical advice that gives every response an added value, a real bonus.

- **From the Principal's Desk:** For this book, I contacted elementary, middle, and high school principals around the country. I sent out questionnaires and conducted numerous face-to-face interviews with experienced administrators in a wide variety of schools (large and small schools; rural, suburban, and urban schools; "wealthy" schools and "poor" schools) from California to Maine and from Washington to Florida. Their "words of wisdom" will give you inside information available nowhere else.

Please know that I have been through many interviews in my teaching career. I've experienced sweaty palms, an upset stomach, and outright nervousness. I've messed up some answers and come through with other responses that really impressed the interviewers. I've heard or responded to all of the questions you'll read about in this book.

I have also been on the other side of the desk and interviewed scores of candidates for teaching jobs. I've interviewed candidates who impressed me within seconds of walking in the door as well as others who didn't even have the common courtesy to shake my hand. I've suffered through long drawn-out soliloquies and been on the edge of my chair listening to mesmerizing and attention-grabbing anecdotes. I've even hired (at least in my mind) some candidates long before the interview was over—they were that good!

In other words, I've experienced both sides of the interview process. Please use my experiences and the information I have gathered from principals and administrators around the country to prepare for your own interview sessions. You'll find this advice valuable whether you are anticipating your first interview ever or whether you have been through a few along the way. I promise you down-to-earth information and a book filled with positive strategies and techniques that can help you land that all-important teaching position.

Keep reading, keep practicing, and remember: You're on your way to an incredibly fulfilling career as a teacher.

FROM THE PRINCIPAL'S DESK:

"There was one interview I'll never forget. A few years ago a young man—I'll call him Jason—came into my office for his initial interview. We exchanged a few pleasantries, and then I asked him the first question: 'Tell me a little about yourself.' He paused for a few seconds and then reached into his briefcase and pulled out an elaborate hand puppet. He slipped the puppet over his right hand, and it was the hand puppet who 'answered' the question. Using a falsetto voice, Jason manipulated the hand puppet—whom he had named 'Bob'—and had 'Bob' respond directly to me. Slightly taken aback (I'd never had a puppet talk to me before), I decided to proceed. So I asked Jason to tell me why he wanted to be a teacher. Again, it was 'Bob' who answered: "'Well, Jason wants to be a teacher because he really likes kids and he knows how to get their attention and he also....' I was still a little stunned—and a little more than amazed—but decided to continue. I asked about two or three additional questions, and each time 'Bob'—in a very animated fashion—told me something about Jason. Finally, after about ten minutes, I could take it no longer. I found a diplomatic way to end the interview, I escorted Jason (and 'Bob') back into the outer office, rolled my eyes at my secretary, and went back into my office to try and recover in time for the next interview. To this day I still have nightmares about that damn puppet."

(One very good reason why you should read this book.)

CHAPTER 1

WHAT YOU NEED TO KNOW ABOUT INTERVIEWS

For most of my life I was a long-distance runner. In high school, college, four years in the armed services, graduate school, and through most of my teaching career, I continued to run long distances. For me, one of the best parts of the day was when I came home from a long day of teaching. I'd throw on a pair of shorts and a T-shirt, lace up my running shoes, and take off for a run of six or eight miles. Occasionally I'd run up and down rolling hills, along dusty lanes, or around the perimeter of a public golf course. Every so often I'd lope over to the local high school to do some interval work on the track. About once a month or so (more in the summertime), I would enter and run a 10K race. Occasionally I would get a trophy or medal for my placement in the race. However, it wasn't the awards that were important to me, but rather the opportunity to run faster than I had in a previous race at the same distance.

I had learned early that the more effort I put into my daily runs the better I would do in the races I entered throughout the year. As a former college coach put it succinctly, "There are only three ways to be a good long-distance runner—run, run, run!"

And guess what: There are only three ways to be successful in a teacher interview— prepare, prepare, prepare! If all you do is put together a resume, send out letters to three dozen schools, and keep your fingers crossed, you may be very disappointed… and jobless! You need to prepare. You need to go the extra mile (or two). Here's the key to getting the teaching job you want: You need to distinguish yourself in some positive way from other candidates vying for the same position(s).

Getting a teaching position must be an active process; it should never be a passive project. Doing what everyone else does (sending out endless batches of applications, correspondence, letters of recommendation, and resumes) will seldom guarantee you a job. You need to set yourself apart from the crowd, distinguish yourself as a candidate of promise, and demonstrate initiative, drive, and enthusiasm. Anything less, and you'll be seen as *one of many* rather than *one of a kind!*

The Themes of a Teacher Interview

When a principal, superintendent, or committee interviews potential teachers, there are several themes they have in mind. While this book provides you with 149 of the most frequently asked questions in an interview (along with suggested responses), it's important to remember that all of these questions and all of the other parts of a teacher interview are centered on eight basic themes. By knowing these universal themes—and by preparing for each one—you can assure yourself of a positive reaction by a prospective employer.

One way to look at each of these eight themes is to imagine each as part of a sales message. Each one is designed to highlight and showcase your skills, abilities, and attitudes in the most favorable light. Each one is designed to separate the mediocre from the good and the good from the great. Everything you do, everything you say, and everything that occurs in a teacher interview is tied to these themes—separately and collectively.

I encourage you to read through these themes. Then, try some of the following:

- Think about each one, and develop a personalized approach to each one.

- Write or record a response—how would your talents, skills, philosophy, and abilities address each theme?

- Take apart your resume, and reassign your personal information to every theme.

- Tell a friend (not in education) how you would present yourself in regards to the themes.

- Write each theme on an index card and carry the cards around with you. Pull the cards out during the course of the day and review them...and review your responses.

In short, prepare yourself to respond—in both word and action—to these key themes and you'll be ready for any interview...and any interview question.

Eight Interview Themes

Every principal or hiring authority wants to know several things about any teacher candidate. Your success in that interview will be based in large measure on how you fulfill each (and all) of the following themes.

1. A Passion for Teaching

When I interviewed principals across the country for this book and asked them to identify the single-most important characteristic in a quality teacher candidate, guess what they all told me? You guessed it: "A passion for teaching!"

Do you have a passion for teaching? How do you demonstrate that passion? What activities, projects, or assignments have you engaged in that demonstrate your passion for and serious commitment to teaching? What have you done that shows you are willing to go the extra mile for students? Did you do something in student teaching beyond the ordinary? Did you do something during your pre-service years that went above and beyond your college's requirements for teacher certification? What truly excites you about teaching? What "floats your boat"?

2. Skills and Experience

One of the first things you need to do in any interview is to establish your ability to do the job. In a nutshell, *Can you teach, and can you teach effectively?* In most interviews, these will be the initial set of questions you'll be asked. Many of these questions will be factual in nature and will provide you with an opportunity to highlight your skills and talents and how they will be used in a classroom setting. This is when you must offer specific information rather than generalities. It is also the time to be completely objective about yourself—with confidence and assurance.

INSIDER TIP

Tony Beshara, who manages a professional recruitment and placement firm in Dallas, Texas, says that the answer to "Can you do the job?" accounts for the first 20 percent of the hiring decision. In short, a candidate must convince an interviewer that he or she is capable of doing the job very early in the interview process.

How do you put together a lesson plan? What do you do when a lesson isn't working? Describe one of your best lessons. What will you bring to the teaching profession? Why should we hire you? Why do you want to be a teacher? What did you learn in student teaching? Please don't make the mistake of assuming that these are easy questions; they are not! They are often asked near the beginning of the interview because they help "set up" the rest of the interview. Positive answers to these questions help ensure the success of the entire interview.

> ## INSIDER TIP
>
> Every interviewer wants to know about the potential and specific benefits you will bring to the school or district. Thus, it is important to give examples of your strengths that relate to the school's needs. For example, instead of saying "I like to teach science," say something like, "I've been known to get even the most reluctant of students interested in science through a 'hands-on, minds-on' inquiry-based approach to science education."

3. Likeability

Here's a basic truth you may find difficult to believe. The most important factor every interviewer is looking for in a candidate is *not* the breadth and depth of his or her skills, education, or talents. It's likeability! In a recent review of more than 100,000 face-to-face interviews, there was not one candidate hired who wasn't, at first, liked by the people doing the interviewing and hiring. You might think that one's personality would be of less value than teaching prowess, but such is not the case. Simply put, people get hired because they are liked.

> ## INSIDER TIP
>
> According to Tony Beshara, "The number of extremely qualified, excellent candidates that weren't hired because they weren't initially liked by the interviewing or hiring authority defies logic and common sense."

What are your three greatest strengths? What are some of your hobbies or free-time activities? How do you handle criticism? How did you handle disagreements with your college supervisor? What makes you the best teacher for this position? Who is the greatest influence on your life? What is the biggest mistake you've ever made? Interestingly, hiring decisions are based more on personality factors than they are on skill factors. You may be the best qualified candidate, but if you aren't the best liked, then the position will probably go to someone else.

4. Student Orientation

Several years ago I was part of a team of people interviewing several candidates for a teaching position. I distinctly remember one young man who spent the entire 45-minute interview talking about his accomplishments, resume, background, and prowess in writing exciting lesson plans. After he left, I remarked to my colleagues that not once, in those 45 minutes, did he ever refer to students. Not once in all that time did he ever use the word "students." It was apparent that he was more interested in presenting himself than he was in teaching students. Candidates without a strong student orientation don't make it any farther in the hiring process. Without that orientation, without that commitment to student life and that desire to work hand-in-hand with youngsters, nobody ever gets hired as a classroom teacher.

How do you motivate an unmotivated student? How do you assess students? Tell us about your toughest student—how did you handle him or her? How do you address cultural diversity in your classroom? What do you enjoy most about working with kids? What are some challenges you've had in working with kids? Besides student teaching, what other work have you done with youngsters? Come to an interview with a strong and sincere student orientation, and you may well walk away with a job offer.

5. Professionalism

You're about to complete a college education. Great! But that doesn't mean your learning has ended. The field of education is changing rapidly, with new technology, standards, and curricula. Your eagerness to continue your education is a key factor in your "hireability." Candidates who assume that just because they have a degree their education is over never succeed in an interview. Any principal or hiring authority wants to know that you are a constant learner—that you are willing to keep learning through graduate courses, in-service programs, on-line seminars and webinars, membership in professional organizations, books, magazines and journals, and a host of other professional opportunities that signal your eagerness to keep your education moving forward.

Where do you see yourself five years from now? What are your plans for graduate school? In what area of teaching do you still need some improvement? Tell me about a book you've read recently. What are the essential traits of a good teacher? Do you belong to any professional organizations? One of my lifelong mantras as a teacher has always been: "The best teachers are those who have as much to learn as they do to teach." Be prepared to demonstrate how you might embrace this quotation in your everyday activities.

6. Management and Discipline

You've probably seen classrooms in which students were orderly, work was productive, and a sense of purpose and direction filled the room. You might also have seen classrooms that were chaotic, disruptive, and seemingly out of control. Maybe you were even a student in one or both of those classrooms at some time. Principals and other administrators are vitally interested in how you plan to manage your classroom. Your management skills and discipline policy will be vitally important in the decision to hire you. Read, research, and review everything you can. Your success here will frequently be a major deciding point.

✔EXTRA CREDIT

According to research, teachers in a typical classroom lose about 50 percent of their teaching time because of students' disruptive behavior. Be prepared to discuss how you would address this issue somewhere in the interview.

To establish a positive classroom environment, share what you will do the first few weeks of school with your students. How do you create and maintain positive rapport with your students? How would you deal with a student who was always late to class? Describe your discipline policy in detail. Describe some classroom rules you would use. To many administrators nothing is more important than a well-crafted discipline policy and a well-articulated management plan. Be prepared to share your thoughts on both.

FROM THE PRINCIPAL'S DESK:

"School districts place a tremendous emphasis on discipline and classroom management. They want to feel confident that you, as a new teacher, have a good, sound, fair method of class management. You can't wimp out in this area."

7. Lesson Planning

A lesson plan is only a guide. A well-designed lesson plan is flexible, subject to change, and reflective of the individual needs of each and every student in the classroom. It provides an outline for the accomplishment of specific tasks, while at the same time allowing for a measure of flexibility in terms of student interests and needs. You need to demonstrate to any interviewer your familiarity with lesson design as well as your ability to tailor lessons to the specific instructional needs of your students. Be prepared to be specific as well as accommodating.

Please relate the process you go through when planning a typical lesson. Please share some ways in which you have assessed students. What are the essential components of an effective lesson? Think of a recent lesson you taught and share the steps that you incorporated to deliver the lesson. Share your process of short- and long-term planning for delivering effective instruction. Think of a lesson that was ineffective or did not meet your expectations—what adaptations did you make to address the lesson? How do you infuse technology to enhance your instruction? It's critical that you provide an interviewer with insight into your lesson planning, delivery, and assessment. Anecdotes and examples must be critical elements of your responses.

8. Flexibility

Can you "roll with the punches"? Can you "go with the flow"? Can you "change directions in midstream" or "bend in the wind"? All these questions have to do with perhaps the most significant attribute of any good teacher: flexibility. Interviewers want to know that they will get the most "bang for the buck"—that you can handle a wide variety of classroom situations, a wide range of teaching challenges, and a wide array of modifications or alterations, all at a moment's notice. Your eagerness to present yourself as someone who can adapt without getting flustered or change without getting upset is a key attribute—an attribute that can often "nail" the interview.

Are you willing to teach at another grade (elementary)? Are you willing to teach another subject area (secondary)? How would you handle a fire drill in the middle of your favorite lesson? If we brought in a brand-new reading series next week, what would you do? Are you comfortable with change? Would you be willing to work in an after-school program? Administrators are always interested in individuals they can use in a variety of situations. The willingness to be flexible and the desire to quickly adjust to change are both positive characteristics valued in any school.

The themes above show up in every teacher interview. Practice them, be prepared for them, and review them on a regular basis. Your preparedness—like that of a long-distance runner—will help you run the extra mile, beat the competition, and set a personal record: getting the teaching position you want!

CHAPTER 2

PREPARING FOR THE INTERVIEW—10 HOW TO'S

Like millions of other people, I enjoy watching the summer Olympics on television every four years. The competition is always first-rate, and the intensity frequently puts me on the edge of my seat. These are world-class athletes at the peak of their athletic prowess. It's often the best against the best.

As a former athlete myself, I know that Olympic athletes don't just get up one morning a few weeks before their events and say, "Hey, I think I'm going to compete in the marathon" and then go out and run 26.2 miles in two hours and five minutes. They have to prepare—for many years—if they have any chance of success in their chosen events. Long hours of practice, months of intense workouts, and years of sometimes painful and excruciating physical conditioning are necessary if an athlete wants to have any chance at winning an Olympic medal. Often the key to success is the amount and level of preparation that occurs long before an Olympic event.

So it is with interviews. The time and effort you put into getting ready for an interview will often be reflected in the success you enjoy in an interview. And take my word for it, an interviewer will quickly know who has taken that time and who has made that extra effort to get ready for an interview. **That effort will be revealed in the depth of the responses and the breadth of experiences brought to the interview.**

Thorough preparation before an interview is just as important as what happens during an interview. Ignore the preparation, and you are essentially "shooting yourself in the foot"—putting yourself at a distinct disadvantage even before you say your first word. World-class athletes prepare for their events years in advance of a competition. Why shouldn't you? You've prepared yourself for teaching; now it's time to prepare yourself for the interview.

INSIDER TIP

Adequate and sufficient preparation before an interview will

- Significantly lower your nervousness and stress during the interview;
- Give you an extra dose of self-confidence;
- Improve your communication skills; and
- Give you the extra edge over your competition.

So here's your training schedule, your preparation "homework" well in advance of any interview. Read the following ten principles and make them part of your training routine. Integrate them into your daily activities, and devote sufficient time to each one. Think of these as your "Interview Decathlon." Spend time "sweating" these ten principles, and you may find yourself with an educational gold medal: a teaching position!

1. Know Your Strengths

You've probably completed several weeks of student teaching. Or you've been involved in a pre-service field experience program through your college or university in which you worked in several different classrooms. Or you may have volunteered for various positions in some of the local schools through the requirements of one of your courses or the outreach efforts of your local student education association. By now, you should have some idea of your teaching strengths. In fact, one of the first things you should do (long before any interview) is to make a list of your strengths, evaluating your personal skills, attitudes, abilities, and accomplishments.

Do you create dynamic and exciting lesson plans? Are you able to handle a room full of rowdy kids? Are you a whiz at integrating technology into any aspect of the curriculum? Can you motivate even the most reluctant of readers to pick up a book? This is a good time to make a list of all your teaching strengths. This information will help generate some useful language you can effectively share with an interviewer.

Make a list—right now—of your six teaching strengths. Share your list with your cooperating teacher, your college supervisor, a favorite professor, and/or a member of your family. Explain why each item on your list is one of your strengths. If you can't vigorously defend one of those items, then cross it off the list and substitute another.

✔**EXTRA CREDIT**

Limit the size of your list to 4–6 items. (It will be easier to remember those specific strengths in an interview than it will be to conjure up a list of 15–20.) Write those strengths down, each one on an individual index card, and carry them around with you in the days preceding the interview. Review them regularly.

One of the most important things you can do in advance of any interview is a self-assessment. This evaluation of your abilities, skills, and talents will help you know what you are good at, and it is essential in communicating that information to interviewers. With this list you will be in a better position to demonstrate how your unique set of abilities can be used to educate youngsters in a particular school or district. Arrive at an interview with your strengths in mind, and you'll arrive with the confidence to do well.

Remember, school administrators are most interested in hiring your strengths. The interview is an opportunity to let a potential employer know what those strengths are and how they will serve the immediate and long-range needs of the school/district. So take the time to self-assess and be ready to share the results of that assessment with any and all interviewers.

- Do your homework! Find out about some of the challenges or concerns that are part of the school or district with which you will be interviewing. What are some of the pressing needs of a particular school? What are some of the issues that occasionally pop up in the local newspaper? Then be prepared to show how your unique abilities can be used to meet those challenges, with examples of how your strengths relate to specific needs.

- Tailor your strengths to the needs of the school/district. For example, if a school is experiencing low reading scores, show how you got kids engaged in an after-school reading program during student teaching.

- Keep your focus on what you can do for the school/district rather than on what they can do for you (give you a teaching job).

- Support your accomplishments with several teaching-related examples of your accomplishments.

2. Do Your Homework

Would you really like to put yourself ahead of the competition? There's one thing you can do (that few of the other candidates will even think of) that can earn you an amazing amount of "brownie points." Simply put, do some research on the school or district. Check out the district or school Web site, and learn everything you can about school/district standards, funding issues, parent involvement, how many students are served, attendance policies, number of schools, size of staff, availability of teacher training programs, results of student achievement tests, description of the facilities, and student support services. Some schools and districts have information packets, brochures, newsletters, blogs, pamphlets, and other informational pieces. Check them out, and learn as much as you can about what makes the school/district unique.

FROM THE PRINCIPAL'S DESK:

"Know as much as you can about my school. Study the Web site. Know why you want to work here and how you can contribute. Do not ask questions about the contract, pay, benefits, etc. It gives the appearance that your primary concern is what you get out of it rather than what you intend to contribute."

One of the best things you can do prior to any interview is to actually visit the school where you will be interviewing. Most administrators will welcome you as a potential teacher candidate. Keep in mind that you are a visitor, and act accordingly. Call the school secretary or building principal and inquire about the possibility of a visit. Ask if it would be possible for you to visit a few classrooms, talk with a few teachers, and see how the school functions on an "average" day. Here are a few items you may wish to note on a visit: the condition of the building, the friendliness of the staff, the enthusiasm of the teachers, the activities of administrators, the ways in which certain lessons are taught, the integration of technology, the noise level in the cafeteria, the behavior management of students, and the emotional climate in selected classrooms.

Whenever possible, try to visit one or more classrooms. If you are allowed, sit in the back of a classroom and casually observe the dynamics taking place. See if you can arrange for an opportunity to informally chat with one or more teachers, either during their planning time or during a lunch break. Tell them that you are a teacher candidate and would like to get some information about the school in advance of an interview. Keep your questions simple and non-direct. Don't ask, "What do you think about those lower-than-average test scores?" Rather, ask something like "What do you like about teaching here?" If the schedule allows, you may be able to casually speak with a few teachers immediately at the end of the school day. As you might imagine, this information will be extremely valuable in your preparations for a forthcoming interview.

- If you are able to visit a school, please be sure to send a thank-you letter immediately after the visit (a letter, not an e-mail). Let the principal know how much you appreciate the opportunity, one or two things that impressed you about the school, and the fact that you are looking forward to the forthcoming interview.

- As part of the interview, be ready to share something about your visit with the interviewer. For example, "During my visit to Indian Hill Middle School last week, I was delighted to see how Smart Boards are being used in the language arts classes. I developed a unique vocabulary review process using Smart Boards during my student teaching experience and would hope to bring my expertise here next year."

✔**EXTRA CREDIT**

Taking the time to research a school or district and taking the time to visit a school in advance of an interview won't necessarily guarantee you a job offer; however, it will put you head and shoulders above all those other candidates who didn't take advantage of this incredible opportunity.

---

3. Practice Makes Perfect

I am constantly surprised at the number of people who don't adequately prepare for a job interview. "It's just a bunch of questions," they say. Or "I'm already qualified; why should I have to study for an interview?" What they often fail to realize is that the amount of work you put into an interview will be quickly noted by any competent administrator. Slough off, and you're history. Make the effort, and you're probably hired!

Answering questions posed by someone you have just met can be harder than you think. Fortunately, this book is crammed with the typical questions that get asked in any teacher interview as well as the best responses to those questions—responses that will get you noticed (positively) and get you hired. Obviously, you must be ready for *every* question and *any* question—and that is one of the major themes of this book.

Here's something you'll be happy to know: Approximately 95 percent of the questions you will be asked in any teacher interview are in this book. Better yet, the appropriate answers to those questions are also in this book. (Obviously, you selected the right book to read!) Read these questions, and practice the answers. Get as close as you can to these questions and answers. All the questions and all the answers came from actual teacher interviews. What you will experience in an interview has been experienced by others. Their experience and wisdom have been distilled in all the chapters of *Ace Your Teacher Interview*. You have a valuable resource here, one that will definitely put you ahead of the competition and give you an added advantage in *any* interview situation.

✔ **EXTRA CREDIT**

Please don't memorize the answers to the questions in this book. If you do, your answers will sound corny or canned. Make these answers yours. Alter the wording, change the emphasis, modify the verbs. In short, turn these answers into *your* answers.

- Every day, practice reading and answering the questions in this book. Know that they have been culled from teacher interviews all across the country. Each of the questions has been asked thousands of times by hundreds of administrators. And guess what? You'll be asked these questions, too.

INSIDER TIP

Practice with the questions in this book, become comfortable with each of them, and then put the responses in your own words. You should be the one answering the questions—not me!

- The key to becoming comfortable with interview questions is to practice answering them over a long period of time. This is not the time to try and cram all this information in your head the night before a scheduled interview (this isn't a final exam, after all). Plan several weeks (at least) or two to three months (if possible) practicing, practicing, practicing.

- Write several of the questions on individual index cards (record an appropriate response on the back of each card). Stuff a set of cards in your pocket or purse. In the spare moments of your day (lunch time, stuck in traffic, before you go to bed), pull out a few cards and review the questions (and answers) so you are comfortable with them all.

4. Promptness

In the process of conducting research for this book, I came across a most amazing (in fact, startling) statistic. Nationally, about 15 percent of all job candidates in business, industry, and education are late for their interviews. That's right, 15 percent! And guess what? Those 15 percent did not get hired! No matter how many excuses they came up with ("My car wouldn't start," "The babysitter arrived late," "I missed the left turn on Jackson Street," "Damn traffic," "I sat behind a snow blower for half an hour," or [the best one of all] "Sorry, I forgot the time"), not a single one of them was offered a job. No way, no how! Arrive late to an interview, and you can kiss your chances of getting hired good-bye.

FROM THE PRINCIPAL'S DESK:

"The negative first impression (of a candidate who is late) is so strong and smelly, it contaminates the entire interview."

When you are late for an interview, you are sending a very powerful message to the interviewer. The message may not be intentional, but it will be extremely clear. It says to the administrator, "I don't plan well," "I'm disorganized," "I'm unpredictable and unreliable," "You're not really all that important," "I don't respect your time," and "You really shouldn't hire me because I can't even do something incredibly simple like getting here on time."

- Make sure you know where you're going. Ask for directions (yes, men, you may have to ask for directions) if necessary. Print out a map or a set of driving instructions from Google or Mapquest.

- Know exactly how long it takes to get there. If your interview is in the early morning or late afternoon, will you have to contend with rush hour traffic? If it is raining or snowing, how will that affect your travel time? Do you have to go through any construction zones or detours? The candidates who make the best impressions are those who take one or two "test runs," driving to the school or district office and noting how much time it takes. Practice the route; you'll be glad you did.

✔EXTRA CREDIT

If you do take a "test run" to the school/district, let the interviewer know about this, preferably in your introductory comments ("Thank you for meeting with me this afternoon, Mrs. Mickleson. I must admit the drive here is quite lovely. I did a practice run last week and was amazed at the profusion of blossoms along Highland Avenue."). This kind of comment signals you as a candidate who knows how to prepare for any assignment, one who plans ahead.

- Plan to arrive about 20–30 minutes early. You don't have to enter the school immediately; rather, you can use this extra time to meditate, relax, do some deep breathing exercises, or quickly review your strengths (see Section 1 of this chapter). Then, plan to walk into the correct office (this may require a pre-interview trip as well) about 7–10 minutes in advance of your scheduled interview.

5. Respect Everybody

Here's something I've often done in interview situations, something that reveals a great deal about a candidate's character. Prior to an interview, I will ask the secretary to engage the candidate in some sort of informal conversation. Or, if time allows, I will ask the secretary to escort the candidate on a tour of the building or grounds. Often, in these situations, the candidate will "let his or her guard down," figuring that this is not part of the actual interview. And, quite often, the candidate will blow it, simply by being discourteous to the secretary, treating her as a subordinate, talking down to her, or ignoring her completely. I would say that about 20–25 percent of the candidates (both male and female) I've interviewed have lost any chance of being hired simply by how they have treated the secretary.

Please consider everyone you meet—from the janitors and secretaries all the way to the curriculum coordinator and superintendent—as important people in the school or district. If you are discourteous or ingenuous to any one, you may find yourself pounding the pavement for another round of interviews. You never know; any person may be part of the interview process.

6. First Impressions

Your mother was absolutely right when she told you, "You don't get a second chance to make a first impression."

INSIDER TIP

There is a considerable bank of research studies that proves that interviewers form an opinion about a candidate in the first 15 to 20 seconds of an interview. Yes, you read that right—the first 15 to 20 seconds!

Suffice it to say it is critical that you establish a good first impression as soon as you walk in the door (even before). The clothes you wear, the style of your hair, the amount of perfume you have on, the condition of your shoes, the firmness of your handshake, and the excitement in your voice will all (collectively) send a powerful message to an interviewer about who you are. Mess up on any one of those initial "contacts," and you will probably mess up the crucial first impression you want an interviewer to have.

It is quite possible you can overcome a poor first impression with a stellar interview, but why put yourself at a disadvantage the moment you walk through the door? Give yourself every advantage, every "brownie point," you can. Knowing that your shoes are shined, that you are making direct eye contact, that your suit was recently dry-cleaned, and that you removed that humongous nose ring from your face will give you the extra confidence you want to do an outstanding interview.

- Be absolutely certain you are dressed professionally. Don't wear your "college clothes"; wear the clothes of a professional educator. For men, that means a coat and tie; for women, it means a classic blouse and skirt. Your attire should be on the conservative side, your shoes should be shined to a brilliant gloss, and your jewelry should be at a minimum. Oh, one more thing: Please cover those tattoos!

- Keep a close eye on your body language. Give the interviewer a firm handshake, and look him or her in the eye in responding to every question. Make sure your feet are planted firmly on the floor and your hands are not stuck in your pockets or smoothing back your hair. Sit up straight in the chair, and lean slightly forward.

- Practice your delivery. Don't speak in a monotone; your voice delivery should be enthusiastic and confident. Be sure to enunciate all your words, and please stay away from any slang.

7. Energy

When I'm interviewing a teacher candidate, I look for one thing above all else. I call it "fire in the belly." I want someone who has a passion for teaching, an excitement about educating kids, and an intense desire to provide the best scholastic experiences for all students they possibly can! Lack that "fire in the belly," and, as far as I'm concerned, you will never be an effective teacher. Lack that "fire in the belly," and you may never find a job as a classroom teacher.

I look for that "fire in the belly" in my college courses as well. Usually, by about the third week of the semester, I can tell who has the "fire" and who doesn't. I can tell who will be a successful teacher because they are excited about learning and they are equally excited about passing along their knowledge to a new generation of learners. Some students take a course because they have to. Others take a course because they are excited about teaching inquiry-based science, they are passionate about a "hands-on, minds-on" approach to the teaching of social studies, or they are energetic about the ways in which literature can enhance any curriculum. It's that latter group who will make the difference in the lives of children.

In your interviews you want to demonstrate that energy and passion. You want the other person to know that this has been a lifelong goal of yours, that the mere act of being with a child in a learning situation is one of life's greatest thrills, and that continuing your education while promoting the education of your students is an incredible experience. You want the interviewer to know, above all else, that teaching is your passion. If it isn't, the interviewer will discover it in the first 15–20 seconds (see the previous section).

> ### INSIDER TIP
>
> Be passionate. Be energetic. Let your words and your body language signal your enthusiasm for teaching. This is your career; this is what you were born to do! Use words like "enthusiastic," "energetic," "motivated," and "passionate" in your responses. Let the interviewer see the spark in your eyes, the forward tilt of your body, and the energy in your words. Above all else, let him or her experience your desire to teach.

Remember: The teacher who gets the job is, quite frequently, the one with "fire in the belly."

8. Process vs. Product

Many candidates make the mistake of assuming that the purpose of the interview is to get a job. Wrong! The purpose of the interview is to "sell" yourself to a potential employer—to demonstrate how your unique skills, talents, and abilities can be effectively used to teach children. I hate to be the bearer of bad news, but the interviewer is not interested in giving you a job; the interviewer is interested in providing the best education possible for the students in his or her school. Whether you are the one to do that is of little consequence to the person doing the interview. Principals and other interviewers want to educate students with the most qualified teachers they can hire; they are not interested in ensuring that you, for example, will "live happily ever after."

In short, don't focus on getting a job offer (simply because that's not what the interviewer is focused on). Rather you should focus on how your particular strengths can be used to ensure a quality-based education program for the students in a particular school. Demonstrate to the person conducting the interview that you know how to teach kids, not that you want a job.

- At every opportunity in the interview, demonstrate how your talents are a "match" for the school. For example, show how the work you've done as a camp counselor can be used to develop an after-school orienteering club. Or show how your love for biology can be used to establish a "stream adoption program" at the high school.

- Be aware of how often you use the personal pronouns "I" or "me." Instead, concentrate on using more "you's" or (more important) "we's."

- Demonstrate how you are willing to become part of an educational team, a team of professionals dedicated to a quality-based education program. Good teaching is a long-term process rather than a quick fix. You aren't there to save them; you are there to contribute to the greater good. At all times demonstrate how you are willing to work *with* them, not necessarily *for* them.

- You need to demonstrate to interviewers that you are more concerned and more interested in their specific agenda than you are in yours. In short, demonstrate what you can do for a school rather than what the school can do for you. Be sure to keep your eyes on the appropriate prize: the benefits you can bring to the school and to the teaching profession. Be sure your responses are school-centered rather than self-centered.

9. Stories—Tell 'Em Stories

Stories have the power to capture the imagination, excite the senses, and stimulate creative thinking. Stories bring life, vitality, and substance to words. They are part and parcel of the human experience and a way of connecting humans as few activities can. And here's the most important element of stories for you, the potential interviewee—stories are better remembered than facts. In other words, candidates who weave stories into the interview are remembered positively. We seldom remember the facts; but we always remember the stories.

For a moment, think about the worst course you took in college. I'm willing to bet that that course was nothing more than a constant barrage of facts and more facts. You had to listen to facts, memorize facts, and regurgitate facts on all those quizzes and tests. Now think about one of your favorite courses. Chances are the instructor took time to share anecdotes, tales, adventures, and vignettes. As a student, you were enthralled with those stories because they brought a topic alive; there was a human connection. You may even recall some of those stories better than you do facts.

Stories are powerful because they establish and build a "bridge" between humans. They allow humans to mentally and emotionally focus on what is being said. In short, you will be remembered more for the stories you share than you will for the facts you tell.

INSIDER TIP

Here's a little secret: In all likelihood a seasoned administrator (e.g., a principal who has served for ten years or more) will have heard many of the same answers to established interview questions a hundred times over—perhaps even more. What they will not have heard is your unique stories, your special anecdotes, and your engaging tales. Provide an interviewer with the same old answers to the same old questions, and you will blend in with the crowd. Spice up your responses with a few stories, and you'll be remembered!

Think about all the educational events and encounters you have experienced since you started college. Turn some of those into stories about yourself that are relevant to issues and concerns critical to teaching success. Make sure they are short and specific. The ideal use of a story is to answer a question and then add a small story to the end of your response. Here's an example:

Q: Why should we hire you?

A: I'm a hard worker and a multi-tasker. When I know there's a job to be done, or several jobs to be done, I go out and do them. While I was in college I was a reporter for the student newspaper, I was on the college soccer team, I was an R.A. in my dorm, I was the parliamentarian for the Student Senate, and I delivered pizzas on the weekends. I was able to do all that and maintain a grade point average of 3.76.

A few key points:

- Don't go overboard on the stories. Develop four to five stories in advance of an interview, and be prepared to share about three to four of them.

- Make sure any stories you share are relevant to the question being asked *and* the needs of the school or district. Don't tell about the time you got disoriented while spelunking in a cave in Puerto Rico over Spring Break— unless it has something specifically to do with the question being asked.

- Don't forget that stories and personal anecdotes will set you apart from all the other candidates applying for the same position. You'll be remembered; they may not!

10. Mock Interviews

At York College of Pennsylvania (where I teach), every education major is required to take *EDU470: Professional Development.* The course is taken the semester prior to student teaching. One of the requirements of that course is that students must participate in a mock interview. We schedule several evenings at one or more of the local schools and invite 20–25 area administrators to join the students in a sit-down dinner and series of mock interviews. Each student is randomly assigned to a principal or assistant principal and must go through a mock interview in exactly the same way as he or she would a real interview. Each student is then evaluated by the interviewer and provided with a list of good points and areas for improvement.

Your college or university might not provide mock interviews as a part of the education program. But that doesn't mean that you can't take advantage of this unique opportunity to practice in a simulated interview situation. Form a support group of other students, and set up a series of mock interviews in which you all get a chance to interview each other. Ask one or more of your education professors if they would be willing to conduct some mock interviews. Invite a local administrator to campus and have him or her conduct some mock interviews for two or three students. Perhaps there is a business person in town, a friend or relative, or someone in the college's career counseling center who would be willing to conduct some mock interviews.

FROM THE PRINCIPAL'S DESK:

"It has been our experience, over the years, that only about 20 percent of all candidates rehearsed their interviews ahead of time."

This may seem like a lot of work; but it can pay off in spades. By going through one or more mock interviews, you will become more comfortable with the entire interview process. You may discover some hidden "quirks" or behaviors that you were previously unaware of (twisting a curl of hair while talking, folding your arms across your chest, or crossing and uncrossing your legs constantly). By becoming aware of these tics ahead of time you can take steps to "cure" yourself of them in advance of a real interview.

- If possible, videotape your mock interview. Then you'll have a visual record of how you did. You'll be able to see yourself as others see you and make any necessary "corrections." Your confidence level will improve, your use of body language can be altered, your speech and language can be changed, and your responses to questions can be shortened or lengthened as necessary.

- In any mock interview, be sure to simulate actual interview conditions as much as possible. Dress the part, and answer the questions as you would in a real live interview. This is not the time to "fake it." This is the time to discover what you might need to improve in order to assure yourself of a positive interview experience.

- Whoever does the mock interview with you, ask him or her to evaluate your performance. You might want to create a self-designed rubric using the ideas and suggestions in this book. You might want to ask a third party to observe the mock interview and provide feedback afterwards. Or you may want to show a videotape to one of your education professors and ask him or her to provide an evaluation as well as suggestions for improvement.

Getting ready for an interview may be just as important as the interview itself. Take the time to practice, prepare, and practice again, and you will give yourself a decided advantage over other potential candidates. The amount of work and effort you devote to the interview *before* it occurs frequently reaps incredible benefits *after* the interview is over.

CHAPTER 3

INTERVIEW FORMATS AND TYPES

One of the mistakes potential teachers often make is to assume that there is one type of interview—the interview in which one person sits across a desk from another person, and one person asks questions for the other person to answer. If you've ever had a summer job or a part-time job in the local community to help pay your college expenses, this is probably the type of interview you're used to.

Yet there is a wide variety of interview types for teaching positions. If you only practice for one type, you may find yourself in an uncomfortable situation when a school or district has a multi-tiered series of several interview types. It's important to be prepared for all the various situations you may encounter. After all, the school or district may be making an annual investment of up to $100,000 (pay, benefits, training) in each new teacher they bring on board. They definitely want to be sure they are getting their money's worth; consequently, they frequently schedule several different types of interviews so that they might get a "true picture" of a potential new teacher. It's both a financial commitment and a personal investment.

What a School or District Wants

When a school or district opens up a position, there are several things they are looking for. Knowing these conditions ahead of time can help you approach each and every interview situation with confidence and assurance. No matter what the interview type or situation, your potential employer wants to know five basic facts about you and every other candidate who applies for the job. These include the following:

- A principal, above all else, wants to know if you are qualified for the job—do you have the basic skills and abilities to be an effective classroom leader? Sure, you have a college education and you've done your student teaching, but so has everyone else. The principal needs to be sure that you have sufficient background and knowledge about educational strategies, philosophies, standards, and basic teaching principles. Almost every candidate who applies for a teaching job has

1) Taken approximately the same courses (irrespective of the college or university attended),

2) Successfully completed a student teaching experience, and

3) Earned a GPA within a very narrow range (typically between 3.3 and 4.0).

In other words, most of the candidates for a teaching position are more alike than they are different. The successful candidate, however, will set himself or herself apart from the crowd by presenting a *unique* set of skills and talents not possessed by the other candidates. These are not the skills and talents listed on a resume or vita; rather, these are the skills and talents often shared in an interview.

- Are you motivated? Are you a candidate who is sincerely excited about teaching and the opportunities for improving the intellectual lives of students? Are you a candidate who can't wait to get in a classroom and make a difference? Are you more interested in the academic possibilities for kids than in getting a job? In short, the job is of less importance that the opportunity to make a lasting difference in students' lives. As a colleague once told me, "You can't fake motivation. You're either in it for the kids or you're in it for the job, and it's quite easy to tell the difference."

✔**EXTRA CREDIT**

Put unbridled enthusiasm in your voice, show unmitigated excitement in your body language, and evidence honest passion in your answers. It's one thing to talk about motivation; it's quite another to demonstrate it.

- Most people in the business world will tell you that the single most critical skill they look for in a potential new employee is his or her ability to work with others. Interpersonal skills are paramount in the success a company envisions. Working as a member of a team is critical to the success of a school, as well. Principals often talk about "everyone being on the same page"—everyone working together toward common goals and shared objectives. You may spend your teaching day inside a room with lots of short people, but you need to be a functional part of one or more larger teams—a grade level team, a subject area team, or a whole school team. Can you fit in with the current culture, and can you make a contribution? Any interviewer wants to know if you'll be a team player.

- Here's a scary statistic: The average classroom teacher will make up to 1,500 educational decisions every day he or she is teaching. Some of those decisions will be minor ones—when to collect lunch money, how to line up in the hallway, when to have recess. Others will be major ones: A student has a grand mal seizure—what do you do? A fire alarm sounds, and two of your students are missing—what do you do? A violent parent enters your classroom threatening you with physical harm—what do you do? Teachers make tons of decisions every day, and a principal wants to know if you are a good decision-maker and/or problem-solver. This problem-solving ability, quite obviously, applies to one's ability to solve educational problems as well as student problems. If you answer every discipline-related question by saying that you would send a child to the principal's office, then your decision-making abilities will be called into question.

- Perhaps the most important factor woven into any type of interview situation is your "likeability factor." Simply put, people want to work with people they like. Do you have an engaging personality, a sense of humor, a spirit, an energy, and an overall "likeability"? Do you get along well with others? Do you go out of your way to help others? A school is a unique community; if you are a "people person," then the community functions well. If, however, you have a negative disposition, a constant frown on your face, or a boring attitude, you will not be contributing to that community. As you will discover later in this book, your "likeability," more than your skills or education, is often the factor that gets you hired—the factor that makes the difference between who teaches and who doesn't.

INSIDER TIP

One of the most important pieces of information an interviewer obtains in any interview is a subjective feeling about the candidate. The questions, conversation, and banter are all geared towards getting at the inner person—the person behind the resume and the brand-new suit. Believe me, the emotional connection is much more important than the courses you took, the people you know, or the grades you got.

Interview Types and Settings

One of the major goals of this book is to provide you with 149 questions you can expect in a teacher interview and responses that will get you hired. But, beyond those questions and answers, it is also important that you are aware of the various formats in which those questions will be asked. Yes, the questions are critically important, but the situation(s) in which they are asked is equally important.

If you were a member of an athletic team in college or high school, you know the significance of "home field advantage." The games or contests you played on your home turf had definite advantages—you knew the playing field because you practiced on it, the home crowd was always on your side, and you were in a "friendly territory." However, whenever you had an "away" game, you found yourself in a foreign place—the playing surface may have been different than what you had at your site, the crowd was definitely different, and the atmosphere may have been negative. Each "away" game or contest was different; each had its own peculiarities, conditions, and atmosphere. Rarely were any two alike.

So it is with teacher interviews. While the questions are the same, the conditions under which they may be asked can differ from school to school or district to district. Each interview is like an "away" game—different territory, different individuals, different conditions.

Basically, there are three types of interviews you will encounter as a teacher candidate. These include screening interviews, performance interviews, and hiring interviews. These interview types and their formats are outlined in the chart below:

Types of Teacher Interviews	Formats
1. Screening	• Telephone • Face-to-face • Electronic • Group
2. Performance	• Teaching a lesson • Role playing/situational • Evaluation
3. Hiring	• One-on-one • Sequential or serial • Panel • Group

Screening Interviews

It is not unusual for schools to be overwhelmed with a large number of applicants whenever a teaching position is advertised. Recently, one elementary school in my local area posted a notice for two elementary classroom teachers. Within the first 48 hours they had nearly 200 applications. After two weeks, there were more than 400. After administrators eliminated the applications from unqualified candidates, they had a "pool" of 30–40 candidates—all of whom (on paper, at least) appeared to be qualified for the positions. They decided to hold a series of screening interviews to pare down the list.

A screening interview is often referred to as a "meet and greet" interview. It is not as structured as a regular interview; instead, it is designed to determine the personality and commitment of selected individuals. These interviews are designed to help principals or other hiring officials make initial decisions on whether they want to further interview a candidate. The main purpose is to narrow the field of applicants to a more manageable number for conducting performance and/or hiring interviews.

Typically, these interviews, due to their intent, are considerably shorter and more general than hiring interviews. They may last 15–20 minutes each, and the questions asked may be more general than specific. That doesn't mean that you should plan any less if invited to a screening interview; your performance in this type of interview will determine whether or not you get invited back for a more formal interview. Do well here, and you'll move forward. Do poorly (or, worse, fail to take this interview opportunity seriously), and you'll be back home sending out another batch of applications.

- **Telephone:** Telephone screening interviews are often used when selected applicants are from out of town or when there are an extraordinarily large number of qualified applicants. Telephone interviews are time efficient and cost effective; they can often be done in ten minutes or less. But these interviews are just as important and just as significant as a face-to-face interview. What you say and how you say it may be even more important in these interviews than they are in face-to-face interviews, simply because there's more value placed on your responses. After all, body language, attitude, and other nonverbal factors do not come into play.

INSIDER TIP

If you anticipate any communication from a school or district (including a phone interview) via your cell phone, make sure your voice mail message sounds professional. No rap music, suggestive comments, obscene language, or "cool" messages that might raise questions about your level of maturity or professional judgment. Use a message your mother would be comfortable listening to.

You would be well advised to conduct some practice interviews via phone. Invite an adult (not a peer) to call you on your phone and ask you 5–7 interview questions from this book so that you can practice your answers as well as your delivery. Ask the person interviewing you to provide some feedback on your responses as well as on how you voiced those responses (e.g., friendly, specific details, enthusiastic). Keep in mind that the intent of a telephone interview is to reduce the number of candidates; your intent is to be included in the final group of candidates invited to a hiring interview. Sufficient practice with this format can help ensure that you will move forward in the hiring process.

- **Face-to-Face:** A face-to-face screening interview is often short, lasting 20 minutes or less. Typically it will involve one or two administrators who will conduct a brief question-and-answer session with you. Rarely will the questions be detailed or in great depth. Typical questions will include those designed to verify the information on your resume; determine if your philosophy of education is consistent with the philosophy of the school; explore your overall knowledge of current trends, practices, or standards; and assess your verbal skills and general demeanor. While this type of interview may seem like a casual conversation you might have at some sort of social setting, it's important to keep in mind that the person or persons conducting this screening are looking for responses in support of the five goals outlined earlier in this chapter.

- **Electronic:** Some schools and districts, in an effort to streamline the interview process, are using electronic screening tools. Essentially, applicants are asked to respond to a select series of questions at a computer terminal. The questions are "scored" electronically and provide administrators with responses in a very short amount of time. One of the advantages is that the electronic questions are all identical for every candidate, thus providing administrators with a way of assessing how well each person responded to the same set of queries. Computer presentations can also note inconsistencies in responses, the time it takes candidates to respond to certain questions (how much thought went into each response), and whether some answers were faked or not (the same question may be asked in several different ways).

  While electronic interviews are more the exception than the rule, that doesn't mean that you shouldn't be prepared for them. The same suggestions for face-to-face interviews apply here as well. Practice with the interview questions in this book, and you'll also be ready for the electronic questions posed on your home or school computer.

- **Group:** One type of screening interview sometimes used is the group interview. In this situation, several candidates are called into an interview room at the same time. Usually there will be several administrators and/or teachers in the room to evaluate all the candidates collectively. Typically, a situation or a scenario (see Chapter 9 for several examples) is presented to all the candidates at the same time. Each candidate is asked to respond to the situation and how he or she might handle it. In some cases, the group of candidates may each be asked to respond to a current topic in education or a controversial issue. Examples may include the following:

"What do you think about 'Race to the Top'?"

"What is your position on 'standards-based education'?"

"Tell us how you would handle a disruptive child in your classroom."

The challenge for this type of screening interview is the fact that you are in direct competition with others. They get to see your performance, and you get to see theirs. The anxiety levels are higher, and the stress factor is accentuated. Everybody is on edge, and everybody is nervous. This is not a fun time. But, if you take the opportunity to practice how you might respond to the scenarios outlined in Chapter 9, you will be putting yourself way ahead of the competition. You will have the assurance of knowing what to expect as well as how to answer those situational questions.

Performance Interviews

Not surprisingly, performance-interview situations are less about the *interview* and more about the *performance*. Typically you are not asked any questions (although a few follow-up questions may be posed); rather, you are asked to demonstrate your teaching expertise in a classroom-type or school-related environment. Administrators want to see if you can put your knowledge into practice. Can you teach? Can you handle the ancillary duties that go along with teaching, and can you take your textbook knowledge and demonstrate how it works in practice?

Keep in mind that the situations you may face in these kinds of interviews are artificial (typically, you won't be doing them in a real classroom with real students); nevertheless, you will need to demonstrate the same behaviors, skills, and talents that would be expected of a teacher on a day-to-day basis. The teaching environment may be contrived, but this opportunity to put theory into practice must never be. Don't try to fake your way through one of these experiences—your lack of knowledge or insincerity will come through loud and clear. Think of this as just one more element—one more day—in your student teaching experience, and you'll be surprised at how well you actually do.

- **Teaching a Lesson:** Many schools and districts are asking teacher candidates to teach a demonstration lesson as part of the interview process. In some cases, you may get to select the lesson to be taught; in others, a subject or specific set of objectives are presented to you in order to craft a unique lesson. Often you'll be asked to teach a full lesson (perhaps 45 minutes in length). At other times you may be asked to teach a mini-lesson (an abbreviated form of a standard lesson). In most cases the lesson will not be taught in a regular classroom, but will be presented in a board room, seminar room, or other location in the administrative offices or a special school location. The audience may include a selection of district administrators and, quite possibly, a few classroom teachers.

You may be told to imagine that the assembled administrators and teachers are a class full of students and that you should teach your sample lesson as though you were teaching it to elementary or high school students. One of my former students was asked to teach a specific music lesson to a group of about six administrators. She said the sight of a half-dozen administrators singing and dancing around a conference room was one she will never forget. Another one of my students was asked to teach a life science lesson incorporating two specific science standards. She developed a "hands-on" lesson using earthworms and still fondly remembers the superintendent getting very ill when asked to handle some of the critters (in spite of that [or because of it], she got the job).

- **Role Playing:** In this type of situation, you may be asked to participate in taking on the role of a classroom teacher with an administrator or teacher taking on the role of another individual. Here you will be asked to show how you might handle one of the common experiences of classroom teachers. For example, you might be asked to be a fifth-grade teacher while one of the administrators in the room takes on the role of an angry parent. You'll be asked to interact with the "parent" to see if you can handle the situation, make appropriate decisions, and problem-solve on the spot. You may be asked to assume the role of a high school social studies teacher who must confront a student with a weapon (say, a knife, for example). An administrator or teacher takes on the role of the student, and you must interact with the "student" to defuse the situation.

These are very stressful situations. All your training and education is on public display. You are being watched by a group of individuals to determine if you can think on your feet and handle some of the many situations that often occur without warning. Take some time to practice several situations, and you will be well-prepared to handle these events with confidence and assurance.

- **Evaluation:** In this interview situation, you may be provided with a set of exams and asked to determine what students have mastered and what you would do with the information in terms of lesson plan design. Often teacher candidates are given a set of student-written assignments and asked to evaluate them using a standard writing rubric. At other times you may be invited to view a videotape of a teacher teaching a specific lesson and asked to evaluate the effectiveness of that lesson or whether the lesson adhered to standard lesson plan design or was in accordance with the standards of a particular subject area. Typically, in these situations, the interviewers have a set standard they are looking for—they want to pare down the list of candidates by giving them all the same "test." Thus, your performance on this evaluation measure will be compared with the evaluation of all the other candidates.

FROM THE PRINCIPAL'S DESK:

"We were undecided between two very qualified candidates. It was only during the demonstration lesson that the differences really emerged. After that, our choice was easy."

Hiring Interviews

Depending on the school or district, you will either go through a screening interview and then a hiring interview or you will go directly to a hiring interview. In short, always expect a hiring interview; it's the last and final step in your journey to becoming a classroom teacher. This is where you make it or break it! Everything in this book is designed to help you be successful in this critical stage—the final chapter in your college career.

Hiring interviews typically fall into one of four categories. In some cases they may include a combination of two or more of the following: One-on-One, Sequential or Serial, Panel, and/or Group. Let's take a brief look at each one:

- **One-on-One Interviews:** This is the most basic of all interviews and the one you will encounter most often in your search for a teaching position. Most of these interviews are conducted by the principal at the school to which you are applying. The interview is most frequently conducted in the principal's office, although some may be held in a conference room or board room. (One of my former students had his one-on-one interview in the principal's car as they were driving from one school across town to another school.)

  This interview is designed to gauge your skills, talents, and abilities as a potential teacher. By this stage of the game, you have made it through a review of your application and resume, any potential screening interviews, and a check of your references. This is where everything you have prepared for comes down to a 45-minute conversation with the one person who will decide whether you get hired. Remember, it's all about *preparation.*

- **Sequential or Serial Interviews:** Sequential or serial interviews are those in which you interview separately with each of several different individuals. Once, when I was interviewing for a reading specialist position, I interviewed with the principal of the elementary school, the principal of the middle school, then the principal of the high school, and finally the superintendent.

You may want to consider that this interview format is simply a string of one-on-one interviews in a row. The interviews may all be held on the same day, or they may be spread out over several days. It is quite likely that you will meet with several different people—all with a stake in the advertised position. The key to success in these interviews is consistency; don't create different responses to the same questions. It is likely that all of the people involved will compare notes and share impressions. Your success will ultimately be determined by your consistency throughout all the interviews.

- **Panel Interviews:** In a panel interview, you will be interviewed by several people at the same time. Typically, the panel will consist of a mix of administrators and teachers. Included may be building principals, assistant principals, people from the personnel office, the superintendent, and selected classroom teachers. Infrequently, it may also include "outsiders" such as college professors, retired administrators or teachers, and/or consultants. Each interviewer will have his or her own unique personality, outlook, set of experiences, and philosophies. As you might imagine, these can be some of the most stressful of all interviews. The key, however, is to respond to each question by directing your response specifically to the person who asked the question. Don't assume that everyone is interested in a specific question (or its specific answer). Make eye contact with the person asking the question, provide your response in 30 seconds to two minutes, and repeat with every other person who asks you a question.

FROM THE PRINCIPAL'S DESK:

"During an interview, our school therapy dog was sleeping under the conference table. The dog had loud and foul gas. The interview committee apologized and explained the dog's important role in our school. The candidate did not skip a beat in her responses. She stayed calm and professional. She laughed with us as we joked about the dog's diet, but did not get distracted or nervous—a true test of character and resiliency."

- **Group Interviews:** These may be the least used of all the interview formats, but that doesn't mean they should be ignored in your preparation process. Here, several candidates are brought into a room at the same time, and they are all presented with the same questions. Talk about a pressure-cooker situation! This is like ancient Rome when the gladiators and the lions were all put into the same arena and the winner was the last one standing. Not only will this situation determine how well you respond to the questions, it will also reveal your interpersonal skills—how well you react and respond to other individuals. Your leadership skills will also be tested in these situations. Are you able to listen to others, build a coalition of ideas, create group harmony, or arrive at mutual conclusions? Most of all, the people doing the hiring want to know if you are a team player. Do you "go it alone," or do you seek out and embrace a common goal, a common direction?

As we've seen, teacher interviews are not always the "standard" one-on-one situations, those times when you sit down with a single individual (typically the building principal) and answer a string of questions. You need to be prepared for any kind of interview or combination of interviews. You can do this as you gather information about the school or district in advance of any scheduled interview. You would do well to inquire about the interview process from a principal, the principal's secretary, the director of personnel, or new teachers currently working in the school. Tap into the expertise of those who have gone through the interview process before you, and use their experiences to your advantage. As with everything else in the hiring process, the more prepared you are, the better you'll do!

INSIDER TIP

If you are given a choice, always select a late-morning interview. Studies have shown that people who interview in the morning are offered a job more often than those who are interviewed in the afternoon. Those same studies have shown that the following days and times for job interviews are the best:

- Best interview days: Tuesdays, Wednesdays, Thursdays
- Best interview time: 10:00–11:00

CHAPTER 4

DON'T MESS UP!
43 MISTAKES YOU CAN'T
AFFORD TO MAKE

This book was written with one goal in mind: to provide you with the most practical information available to help you secure a teaching position. In order to do that, I surveyed all the literature on recruiting and hiring, interviewed school administrators throughout the country, surveyed principals from coast to coast, and tapped into the collective wisdom of teachers just like you who have successfully negotiated the interview process and obtained the job of their dreams. This book has been built on the success of others who have gone before you as well as on the "inside secrets" of those who do the actual interviews. What you have in these pages is a distillation of some of the best experience and thinking on teacher interviews to be found anywhere.

Not only did I want to provide you with the most practical information on how to have a successful interview, I also wanted to let you know about some of the mistakes teacher candidates typically make—mistakes that often doom their chances, cost them the job, or derail their chances for employment. These are the mistakes that pop up often enough that they deserve their own chapter. While the rest of this book is on the "positives" of successful interviews, this chapter will focus on the "negatives." That's simply because these events happen so frequently and in so many interviews across the country that they seem to be persistent, a virus that far too often sneaks its way into an interview and "contaminates" any chance you have of getting hired.

But there's one important thing about this list. As you look over these typical and common "boo-boos," you will note that they all have one thing in common—they can all be controlled by you! Each of these interview mistakes is under your control, your supervision, your influence. That's right, each of these interview mistakes is under your control! You can choose to ignore all of these, or you can choose to do your "homework" and prevent any one of these from sneaking its way into your interview. You have the power to address each and every item on this list. People before you have made these mistakes, and they are probably going to continue to make them. Let their mistakes be your guidance for a most successful interview.

A. Pre-Interview

1. Uses a Cell Phone

Here's a fact of life: Your cell phone will not help you get a job, but it does have the potential to make sure you never do. Here's the best piece of advice I can give you, and I know it will be painful for some: Leave your cell phone in your car. *Do not* take it into the school, and *do not* take it into the interview. Don't even think about it. If you spend any time on your cell phone while in the school or in the interview, you will be sending a very powerful negative message to the interviewer: My business is more important than yours.

> ### FROM THE PRINCIPAL'S DESK:
> "I was interviewing a candidate one day, when his cell phone rang. He stopped speaking and answered the call. After about a minute he put his phone back in his pocket. We continued the interview until five minutes later, when his phone rang again. Once more he stopped talking and answered the call. When he was finished, I got up and showed him the door. Bottom line: I will not tolerate impoliteness."

Oh, one more thing: Don't wear a Bluetooth to an interview. And the same goes for your iPod.

2. Is Tardy

First impressions count! Get to the interview late, and you will make one of the worst impressions ever. It makes no difference what your reasons are or what kinds of excuses you use (one of my favorites—"Your secretary gave me really lousy directions."). If you are late, you are out! In case you think this is not a common occurrence, one research report showed that 50 percent (**yes, 50 percent!**) of job candidates were tardy for their interviews. If you really want the job, be on time. Don't be rude, be punctual!

3. Makes a Bad Impression in the Waiting Area

Don't talk on your cell phone, listen to your iPod, play a game of Solitaire on your laptop, check your e-mail, smoke, or chew gum. Instead, read an educational book, review your interview notes, or (if appropriate) engage in a pleasant conversation with the secretary or receptionist. Even before the actual interview starts, you are being evaluated by others. Be a professional, so do something professional.

B. Personal

4. Displays Poor Social Skills

If you don't know how to carry a conversation with all the people who work in a school—janitors, secretaries, teacher aides, cafeteria workers, other administrators, volunteers, etc.—then you are in trouble. Treat everyone as important to the functioning of the school; never bad-mouth or talk down to anyone. Have a pleasant smile and a courteous greeting for everyone you meet.

5. Presents a Poor Appearance

Okay, here's your basic list: Don't wear clothing inappropriate for an interview, get rid of any body jewelry (the lip ring is cute, but you won't impress any principal with it), cover up any and all tattoos, don't use an excess of perfume or after-shave lotion, take a bath or shower (with real soap) the morning of the interview, use a deodorant, go light with the jewelry and the makeup, get a haircut or a hair styling, trim your nails (fluorescent blue nail polish is out), brush your teeth and use a mouthwash, ditch the gum and cigarettes, and put on your best smile. One more thing: Don't drink any alcohol before an interview. You definitely won't be doing yourself any favors.

FROM THE PRINCIPAL'S DESK:

In the course of my research for this book, I interviewed scores of principals from every part of the country. When I asked each of them for the #1 most common mistake teacher candidates make, more than 90 percent of them replied, "Unprofessional dress or appearance."

6. Maintains Poor Eye Contact

When someone asks you a question, look that person straight in the eye and provide an answer. Candidates who glance around the room, look down at the floor, avoid the eyes of the interviewer, or stare at the aquarium behind the principal's desk are seen as insecure, unsure, and unconnected. Eye contact is the surest way to establish rapport with someone and to maintain good lines of communication.

7. Offers a Limp or Overly Firm Handshake

This may seem like silly advice, but please practice your handshake. Give a limp handshake, and you will be seen as insecure. Give an overly powerful handshake, and you'll be seen as domineering. Also, save the "high fives" and "fist bumps" for your fraternity buddies or friends.

8. Lacks Confidence

If you don't walk into the school or into an interview room with a degree of self-confidence, you will be putting yourself at a disadvantage. Practice all the tips, ideas, and strategies in this book, and you'll have the confidence you need to impress an interviewer and do well in the actual interview.

INSIDER TIP

According to the latest research from professional interviewers, when we meet someone for the first time, 93 percent of the overall impression formed comes from nonverbal messages, not from what is actually said. How we look when we meet an interviewer sends a powerful message, one that establishes a tone (positive or negative) for the actual interview.

C. Speech

9. Communicates Ideas Poorly

One of the first rules prospective lawyers learn in law school is that a good lawyer "never asks a question in open court that he or she doesn't already know the answer to." By practicing with the questions in this book, you will know how to respond to each one. You will know what to expect and how to answer. By practicing with these questions, you will discover very few "surprise questions" in an interview.

10. Uses Poor Grammar

"Ya know what I mean?" "Like it was totally cool, man." "He was so full of it." "She was freakin' out of her mind." "Like, O.K." "I mean, he was one bad-ass dude." Hey, you've spent four years in college. You've taken English courses and at least one speech course. Don't blow your chance for a job by using inappropriate grammar. Clean it up. Now.

11. Is Inarticulate

Speak clearly and understandably. Makes sure you can be easily heard from a distance of five or six feet (the average distance between a person behind a desk and one in front of the desk). Mumbling your words or using a slurred speech pattern will doom your interview as well as your potential performance in a classroom.

12. Talks Too Much

This is not a time to tell an interviewer everything you know about education. It is, quite simply, an exchange of information. In other words, don't take over the conversation. Know when to listen. Know when to talk. Know when to shut up—and then shut up!

INSIDER TIP

Most professional interviewers advise that the ideal answer to a question should be no shorter than 30 seconds and no longer than two minutes.

13. Argues with the Interviewer

Can you believe that, in order to make a point, some candidates actually argue with the interviewer? I have one word for interview arguments: Don't!

D. Presentation

14. Gives Canned Answers

Practice with the questions and answers in this book, but don't memorize them. These questions are the ones asked in every interview, and most administrators have heard similar responses to each one. Put these responses into your own words, your own thoughts, and your own philosophy. Massage these responses so they sound like they belong to you.

✔ EXTRA CREDIT

When asked a question, allow one to three seconds before you give a response. That "wait time" gives an interviewer the impression that you are thoughtful and poised (and that you actually listened to the question). There will be less likelihood your response will be viewed as memorized or "canned."

15. Has a Relaxed or Informal Attitude

An interview is serious business. Your future is often dependent on what you do during the 45 minutes of an interview. Treat it as seriously as you would the teaching of students. If you appear lackadaisical, lazy, or noncommittal, you'll never be taken as a serious educator.

16. Is Not Focused

Jumping around from topic to topic, not completing an answer, losing your focus, stopping and starting several times when responding to a question, and a plethora of incoherent or incomprehensible thoughts will surely doom any interview. Trust me, it happens—more than you might imagine—and, if it continues, it is a sure sign that the interview will probably end prematurely.

17. Gives Defensive or Aggressive Answers

Don't come to an interview with an attitude or a "my way or the highway" philosophy. This is the time to make an impression, not to make a point. If the interview becomes confrontational, then it is certain that it will also become done!

18. Is Arrogant

Interviews are stressful situations. You'll sweat a little more, your blood pressure will go up a little more, and your nervousness will increase a little more. Some people try to compensate for these natural physiological reactions by being arrogant or haughty. They try to maintain control of their emotions with a superior attitude or imposing personality. These are, as you might imagine, not behaviors principals want in their schools, nor are they behaviors that lead to good morale or team building among teachers. It's one thing to be confident; quite another to be arrogant. Be the former, not the latter.

19. Has No Questions for the Interviewer

You may be surprised to learn that many professional interviewers believe that asking questions in an interview is much more important than answering them. By asking your own questions, you are demonstrating an interest in that particular school or district. If you've done your homework properly, you will be able to tailor those questions to the specifics of a school ("On my informal visit here last week I noticed many teachers using literature circles. What are some of the benefits you've seen with literature circles?"). Don't make the fatal mistake, when asked if you have any questions, of saying, "No, not really. I think we've covered pretty much everything."

INSIDER TIP

Always try to ask one or two questions directly related to the interviewer. "I noticed that you're teaching an evening course at Ivory Tower Tech. What are some of the things you've gained from that experience?" or "In reading the school's Web page I saw that you got your master's degree in reading from Slippery Slope College. Is their program still as challenging as ever?"

20. Has a Negative Attitude

Listening to someone with a negative attitude is always a drain—emotionally, psychologically, and personally. The same holds true for someone who is always bad-mouthing other people. Principals don't hire "bad attitudes"; they want people with a positive outlook, a good sense of humor, a sunny disposition, and an engaging personality. They want to hire teachers who will be good role models for students. Negative people are not part of that dynamic.

INSIDER TIP

Be a gracious guest. If the interviewer is late for the interview, shrug it off. If the interviewer answers the phone several times during the interview, just let it be. If people stick their head into the room several times during the interview, don't let it rattle you. If you show any signs of irritation or over-reaction over these little "slights," you'll never get a job offer.

21. Gives Short, Vague, or Incomplete Answers

When asked an interview question, it is expected that you will provide the interviewer with some specific details and explanations. Very rarely will you ever be asked a question that requires a simple "Yes" or "No." It's equally important that you provide a very specific response. Answers such as, "I'm not really sure" or "Wow, I never thought about that" will not win you many friends and will, most certainly, not enhance your "hireability."

✔**EXTRA CREDIT**

You may be asked a question that is difficult to answer. Here's one way of responding: If you don't know the answer, simply say so. Don't try to "wing it." Make no apologies. Smile. Say something like "I'm afraid I don't know enough about that topic to answer. However, I would like to get back to you with a response." Then, when you write your thank-you letter after the interview, address that question and offer a subsequent answer ("I wasn't able to respond to your question about whole-class assessment, but I just found an interesting study that showed how....").

22. Is Unprepared

Principals will know, within the first two to three minutes, if you haven't prepared for the interview. Simple solution: Be prepared! That's why you bought this book, isn't it?

FROM THE PRINCIPAL'S DESK:

"It astounds me at times when candidates come to interviews unprepared and not dressed professionally."

E. Knowledge

23. Doesn't Know Current Educational Issues

Are you up to date on the most current educational trends, issues, and concerns? Do you know what's "hot" in the field of teaching? Are you reading a variety of educational journals and professional publications? Are you aware of any current or pending educational legislation in your state? If you can't answer "Yes" to all of those questions, then you have some homework ahead of you. Take the time to speak with your education professors outside of class. Get copies of some of the latest education magazines from your college library, and read them cover to cover. If possible, attend a local or regional education conference and learn as much as you can about current issues. Do a Google search or follow an education blog to discover what challenges teachers are facing and how they are dealing with those challenges. Get up to date on the issues, and you will impress the interviewer. Failure to do so will certainly doom your chances.

24. Is a Know-It-All

Ever since I first began teaching more than 40 years ago, I have
one simple philosophy: "The best teachers are those who have as
as they do to teach." Simply stated, good teachers are good learners.
for a minute that just because you're about to get your college degree
everything there is to know about teaching. I don't...and you certainly n't! Come
into an interview thinking you have the answers to all of education's challenges,
and you will soon find yourself on the outside of the school looking in. Here's the
reality: I'm not an expert and neither are you. I still have a lot I'd like to learn. So
should you. Your learning doesn't end with graduation; indeed, it's just beginning.
Let a principal know that learning is a lifelong mission (rather than a completed
task) for you, and you'll score major points in an interview.

25. Displays No Knowledge of the School or District

Give yourself an advantage. Do your homework (many will not), and conduct some
research on the school or district. What is their overall philosophy? How many
schools do they have, and where are they located? Do most of the teachers have
master's degrees? How much does the local community support the school/district?
How many students are in the school/district? Where did the principal go to school?
Whenever possible, visit the community and the school in advance of an interview.
Get to know them and they, very likely, will want to get to know you.

FROM THE PRINCIPAL'S DESK:
"One question I *always* ask in a teacher interview is, 'What do you know about our district?'"

26. Asks Inappropriate Questions

There are two types of questions you should never pose in an interview. Never
ask about salary matters, and never ask about benefits. In the first place, you're
asking the wrong person (or persons), because those are matters handled by the
local bargaining unit (if any). In the second place, by asking those questions you're
indicating that you are more interested in the financial rewards of teaching than you
are in the actual act of teaching. That's a bad impression.

7. Personality

27. Tells the Interviewer What He or She Thinks the Interviewer Wants to Hear

You're not being very honest—with yourself or with the interviewer—when you give answers you don't believe in. One of the purposes of the interview is to share your philosophy, your training, and your beliefs about teaching with one or more people. Your answers have to come from the heart as much as they do the mind. Your objective is not to try and satisfy an interviewer; rather, your objective is to showcase how your unique talents and attitudes will make a positive difference in the educational lives of students in that particular school. Please don't kid yourself that if you answer a question the way you think it should be answered you'll get the job. If you don't practice the answer and if you don't sincerely believe in the answer, then it will show. And the interviewer will know it.

28. Believes His or Her Methods and Philosophies Are the Only (or Best) Ones

They aren't! Get over it.

29. Isn't Flexible

One of the most important skills any teacher can have is flexibility. Without it, you'll never survive in a classroom. Equipment breaks down, colleagues get sick, somebody throws up on your lesson plans, a guest speaker doesn't show up, you slip on the ice and break your ankle in three places (yes, that happened to me), the hamster escapes from his cage, there's a fire drill right in the middle of your fantastic PowerPoint presentation on the Reformation, and the list goes on. Flexibility—being able to roll with the punches—is key to your success as a classroom teacher. If you can demonstrate that you aren't easily flustered or thrown off your game plan by the inevitable interruptions, miscues, and unplanned events of classroom life, then you will have a much greater likelihood of being hired.

INSIDER TIP

Several studies have shown that the ability to "embrace change" is one of the most significant predictors of employment success. It is essential that you persuade an interviewer that you are able to adapt and flow with change. (This can be easily done through the use of personal stories or anecdotes.) The ability to deal with change is critical to a successful interview and a successful career as a classroom teacher.

30. Displays Negative Body Language

As you'll learn in Chapter 5, your body language sends a very powerful message to any interviewer. Slouch in your chair, fold your arms across your chest, fiddle with the keys in your pocket, never smile, keep crossing and uncrossing your legs, never make eye contact, scratch various body parts, run your fingers through your hair, yawn, tap your toes, and give a "limp-wrist" handshake, and the interviewer knows a lot about you (unfortunately, it's all negative) without even listening to your responses to his or her questions. Your body sends a very powerful message—be sure it's the right one (a good reason to read the following chapter).

31. Demonstrates Poor Listening Skills

Remember that an interview is a conversation. In any effective and successful conversation, people must talk and people must listen. If you spend too much time focused on what you want to say and not enough time on listening to what the interviewer is saying, then you'll be involved in a non-productive interview. It's important to establish a rapport with the person interviewing you. The best way to do that is to listen carefully to what he or she is saying or asking. Smile, nod, or give some physical indication that acknowledges what you are hearing, and you'll solidify the rapport essential to a productive interview.

32. Is Unwilling (or Unable) to Accept Responsibility

Good teachers are responsible. Poor teachers are always willing to accuse others or make flimsy excuses for their own behavior. If you make a lot of excuses, then the message you are sending is that you are an irresponsible person—and principals don't want irresponsible teachers in their schools. Here are some of the excuses teacher candidates have offered during interview sessions. I hope none of these came from you.

- "My professors obviously didn't know what they were talking about."
- "I got a lousy education."
- "The principal at Drowning Sheep Elementary wasn't very helpful."
- "Nobody told me what to do."
- "I forgot."
- "Hey, it wasn't my fault."
- "It was a stupid school."
- "What do *you* think I shoulda done?"
- "The other teachers were just a bunch of snobs."

- "That's not what it said in the textbook."
- "My cooperating teacher was a jerk."
- "My college supervisor was a jerk."
- "They never gave me a break."

✔EXTRA CREDIT

If you made a mistake or blew a lesson during student teaching and are asked about it, own up to it. But also share 1) how you corrected the situation, and 2) what you learned as a result of the experience.

---

33. Has No Sense of Direction

If you have no long-term goals, no sense of direction, no idea where you will be or what you will be doing ten years from now, then you'll have a difficult interview experience. Interviewers want to know if you have a plan, a detailed roadmap of where you would like to be in the future. Education is never a destination; it is always a journey. And if you don't know where you're going, then you'll never know when you get there. If all you want is a job, then you'll be like thousands of other potential teachers—always looking for one. If you have a specific plan of action for your career—beyond the current job opening—then you will grab the attention of an interviewer.

34. Lacks Confidence and Self-Esteem

You're going to feel nervous just before an interview. You're going to have one or more butterflies flitting around in your stomach during the interview. And you're going to ask yourself a thousand questions after the interview. These apprehensions are quite natural and have been experienced by millions of teachers who, just like you, were trying to get ready for that all-important interview. But, by practicing the techniques and suggestions in this book, rehearsing your responses to the sample questions, and participating in a few mock interviews, you can gain the confidence and self-assurance that will steel you through the entire interview process. If it makes any difference, know that the person who will be interviewing you has gone through more than one interview himself or herself. He or she knows the feelings, the emotions, and the uncertainty. Interviewers have been there and done that. Walk in with a smile on your face and a determination to show the interviewer that you have prepared for this interview, and you'll have the confidence you need to succeed.

35. Is Discourteous, Ill-Mannered, and Disrespectful

Mind your manners! Be courteous! Respect everyone! End of lecture.

G. Other

36. Has "Not My Job" Syndrome

Show that you are willing to take on any and all assignments that may come your way. Don't tell an interviewer about all the duties and assignments you'd rather not be doing ("Hey, I'm a teacher, and the only thing I do is teach kids!"); rather, let him or her know how you are willing to "go the extra mile" and do a little bit more than you're asked. I hope you're not surprised to discover that teachers do more than just teach—they have bus duty, hall duty, cafeteria duty, bathroom supervision duties, after-school duties, study hall duties, tutoring duties, and a whole host of other duties that frequently take place outside the four walls of a classroom. Ultimately, principals want people who will make their job a little easier, not more challenging (see Chapter 6).

37. Blames Students

Never blame students for the fact that a lesson went wrong, you received a low evaluation in student teaching, or the third grade Christmas play fell flat on its face. Don't even try this! It may be difficult to believe, but blaming kids pops up in more interviews than you would care to imagine. This will be a certain "nail in your coffin" if you assign blame for your shortcomings, faults, or failures to the students you worked with in student teaching or in your field experience requirements. If you blame students in an interview, it's certain you will blame them in a classroom. And nobody wants that!

38. Lacks Passion

You'd better be excited about teaching and kids! If you don't demonstrate any excitement or enthusiasm about the education profession in an interview situation, how are you ever going to share that passion with the students in a classroom environment? You're in teaching because you want to make a difference in the lives of youngsters—show it, say it, radiate it in every response to every question. Be excited about teaching, and the interviewer will be excited about you!

> ## FROM THE PRINCIPAL'S DESK:
> "Two keys to a successful interview: Show excitement about the profession, and exude a love of children."

39. Engages in Inappropriate Behaviors

These have all happened in teacher interviews—more than you could ever imagine. Don't let them happen in yours.

- Is late.

- Plays with objects on the interviewer's desk.

- Cracks an off-color joke; cracks several off-color jokes.

- Uses sexist language ("Well, you know women!").

- Uses the first name of the interviewer.

- Is way too friendly ("Hey, dude. What's happenin'?").

- Makes comments about the interviewer's family ("Your wife is cute. Are those your kids?").

- Challenges the interviewer's ideas ("You don't really believe that, do you?").

- Doesn't shake hands.

- Keeps watching the clock or checking his or her watch ("Are we almost done, yet? I have to pick up my boyfriend.").

- Talks too loudly; talks too softly.

- Scratches his or her body…often (Think: lice).

- Has a severe case of halitosis.

- Hasn't been near a bar of soap in, say, a week.

40. Volunteers Inappropriate Information

Don't share any of the following:

- "I'm taking medication for my depression."

- "I'm taking the pill, so I won't be having babies for a while."

- "My parents are getting a divorce."

- "I'm thinking about coming 'out of the closet.'"

- "I'm a Republican."

- "My boyfriend is in jail for about the next six years."

- "I'm pregnant."

- "I'm Jewish."

- "I'm 42 years old."

- "I've got this really cool dragon tattoo on my shoulder and this really neat navel ring. Wanna see?"

You should not volunteer or share any information regarding politics, age, religion, marital status, sexual orientation, family, mental or physical health, sexual behaviors, body art or body decorations, receipt of unemployment benefits, spouse's legal issues, or children. Oftentimes, too much information is simply that…too much information.

41. Is Dishonest or Deceptive

Dishonest or deceptive individuals are easy to spot. They rarely give straight answers to questions. They are evasive about events in their lives that might have negative implications (being fired from a job, taking a decrease in salary, switching jobs frequently). They appear to have something to hide, something to conceal. They often change the subject when the conversation becomes too personal. And they often shift their gaze around the room, seldom making eye contact when answering questions. Any of these behaviors will quickly grab the attention of the interviewer…in a most negative way.

42. Is Self-Centered

Here's a harsh reality: The interviewer is not interested in hiring you. He or she is interested in hiring the best-qualified individual for the position. If it is you, then that is fine by the interviewer. If it is someone else, then that's also fine for the interviewer. In short, *you* are not the commodity; you just happen to be the person sitting across from an interviewer who wants to fill an open slot in his or her faculty. You can assist the interviewer tremendously by keeping the focus off you and directly on the contributions you can make to the welfare of the school. If you frequently use "I" or "me" in your interview, you will send a negative message to the interviewer—a message that you are the most important part of the equation. However, when you use "you" and "we" throughout the conversation, then you are shifting the emphasis to where it should be—away from *you* and on to *them*.

FROM THE PRINCIPAL'S DESK:
"Keep all your answers kid-centered. You can't go wrong there."

43. Doesn't Follow Up

Read Chapter 13. Please.

CHAPTER 5

PUT YOUR BEST FOOT FORWARD (THE NONVERBAL EDGE)

INSIDER TIP

According to several professionals in human resources, most of the hiring decision about a specific candidate is typically made in the first three to five minutes of a face-to-face interview, even though the entire interview may last several times that long.

If you read the statement above, you will quickly gather that your success in an interview situation—particularly in a screening interview (please see Chapter 3)—is made very quickly. What you say, how you say it, and what you do are quickly assessed, quite often before you even have a chance to respond to the first two or three interview questions. Yes, first impressions do make a difference! As I'm sure your mother told you many times, "You don't get a second chance to make a first impression!"

While the bulk of this book is focused on the typical questions you will be asked, and the answers that will set you apart from everyone else, you also need to be aware that how you present yourself—particularly in the initial minutes of an interview—will have a significant bearing on whether you move forward or not. Even before you sit down in the interviewer's office to answer the first formal question, your interviewer has already begun making up his or her mind about you. What you do (and how you present yourself) in the first five minutes of an interview may have more significance than what you might say in the last 40 minutes of that interview.

INSIDER TIP

Communication studies reveal that approximately two-thirds of what is communicated from one person to another is primarily through nonverbal cues. We frequently learn more about people through nonverbal means than verbal ones.

The Essential Seven

Let's take a look at the seven most critical nonverbal behaviors that can establish you as a candidate worthy of an interview (or two) and one worthy of a position with a particular school or district. But first, a word of warning! You might look over this list and my suggestions and say, "These are all fuddy-duddy ideas. They don't apply to me." But indeed they do. Keep in mind that teaching, as a profession, still tends to be a little on the conservative side—your appearance, your speech, and your behavior as a teacher are often measured by a different set of criteria than those of, say, a carpenter, a politician, or a burger-flipper at the local fast-food restaurant. Teachers are often evaluated with a different set of expectations or values than those in other professions.

RULES FOR TEACHERS

You may find these rules for teachers (circa 1915) interesting. You should be pleased to learn that they are no longer being enforced (at least to my knowledge):

- You will not marry during the term of your contract.
- You are not to keep company with men.
- You must be home between the hours of 8:00 p.m. and 6:00 a.m. unless attending a school function.
- You may not loiter downtown in ice-cream stores.
- You may not travel beyond city limits unless you have the permission of the chairman of the board.
- You may not ride in a carriage or automobile with any man unless he is your father or brother.

- You may not smoke cigarettes.
- You may not dress in bright colors.
- You may under no circumstances dye your hair.
- You must wear at least two petticoats.
- Your dresses must not be shorter than two inches above the ankle.

You may say that the differentiated expectations for teachers are unfair, and you'd probably be right. But it's the way things are...and the way things will continue to be for quite some time. Pay close attention to the suggestions in this chapter. They come from a wide range of administrators from across the country, and they have been used in countless teacher interviews for many, many years. While you may not like them, you ignore them at your peril! You want to impress any interviewer from the first time he or she lays eyes on you all the way until you leave the parking lot after the interview is over. Your first impression (and your final impression) carries significant weight in your overall evaluation. Think of these ideas as a blueprint for success. Mess up on any one, and you may mess up your interview...and your career.

Here are the seven nonverbal behaviors you need to work on before and during any interview:

1. Clothing and attire
2. Nervousness
3. Enthusiasm
4. Body language
5. Body parts and adornment
6. Eye contact
7. Voice

1. Clothing

What you wear conveys an image. If you tend to wear ratty T-shirts, dirty jeans, and worn-out moccasins, people will get an instant impression of you long before they speak with you. In our society, what people wear conveys an instant first impression. Your ratty T-shirt may have absolutely nothing to do with who you are as a person, but when people see that shirt they will assume that you are unkempt, unconcerned with conventional dress, and a generally messy person. You may be something entirely different, but the general public still evaluates people on how dressed up (or dressed down) they are. Is that unfair? Yes. But that's one of the stark realities of life.

Basically, you want to dress for success. How you dress will be the first thing an interviewer or committee sees, and it is your best opportunity to get the interview off to a positive start. When in doubt about what to wear, always go with conservative, mature, and professional.

✔ EXTRA CREDIT

In your visits to schools, and during your student teaching experience, make a note of the outfits school administrators wear ("Casual Fridays" don't count). Notice what both men and women administrators (principals, assistant principals, superintendents, curriculum coordinators) wear during the day, and model your interview wardrobe accordingly.

Men: Plan to wear a sport coat and a good pair of slacks (both recently dry cleaned). It's okay to wear a suit, but a navy blue sport coat with medium gray or tan slacks is a classic duo. Stay away from black, a color that denotes very formal attire or a great deal of power. The style of your outfit should be well-tailored—again, with a slight lean towards conservatism. Try to select a coat and slacks that are of a natural fiber—cotton or wool—rather than a synthetic blend.

Select a shirt color that is lighter than the color of your coat (black or purple shirts are definitely unacceptable). White or light blue Oxford shirts are good choices. Wear a tie that coordinates with your shirt; solid colors or stripes are always preferred over loud or painted ties. The tie should be knotted neatly and pulled right up to your collar. Don't wear any pins or other adornments on your jacket. Make sure your socks are color-coordinated with your tie.

Wear standard dress shoes (with laces) instead of loafers, sandals, moccasins, or work shoes. Check the heels to be sure they are not worn down. And always—I mean *always*—shine your shoes the night before an interview. I have known far too many candidates who were derailed simply because they didn't take the time to shine their shoes.

FROM THE PRINCIPAL'S DESK:

"The first thing I check is whether or not the candidate's shoes are shined. If they are, he or she is 'in.' If they aren't, then for me the interview is essentially over. If a candidate can't take care of the little things—like shined shoes—how is he or she going to be able to take care of the big things, like teaching kids?"

Women: Again, aim for a conservative style. Your best choice is a suit with a matching skirt and jacket. You may choose to wear a skirt and blouse of one color with a jacket of another color. Bright colors such as reds and yellows are inappropriate; keep your color selection to blues, browns, and grays whenever possible. As with men, you should opt for natural fiber suits rather than synthetics. Make sure the suit is well-styled and well-tailored. Don't wear a pantsuit; it often conveys informality. The same goes for miniskirts.

Your blouse is a critical choice in your interview outfit; do not skimp on this article of clothing. Select a blouse of quality fabric; cotton is always suggested. Stay away from blouses with ruffles, oversized collars, frills, or loud colors. And, ladies, please select a modest blouse rather than a revealing or off-the-shoulder one. Just as interview committees will talk about men's shoes, they often talk about a woman's neckline. Show too much cleavage (or any cleavage, for that matter), and your chances of getting a teaching job will be close to zero.

FROM THE PRINCIPAL'S DESK:

"There were three of us—all men—on a committee interviewing several teacher candidates. One young lady came in wearing a skirt that was slit all the way up the side. About three minutes into the interview, she crossed her legs exposing her right leg almost up to her underwear. At that point I leaned over the table and politely told her that she should have a conversation with her mother about appropriate attire and appropriate dress. I then escorted her out of the room and called in the next candidate."

Select your accessories with extreme care. Keep your jewelry to a minimum (a ring on every finger is a little over the top). A classic necklace, small earrings, and a single ring are often sufficient. Don't wear a lot of flash and sparkle. You don't want an interviewer focused on your jewelry collection; you want him or her focused on you.

Also keep your makeup to an absolute minimum. Please don't overdue the eye makeup; go lightly on the mascara and eye liner. Your lipstick should be pink, red, or coral—black is a no-no. It's okay to use fingernail polish—shades of red are fine; shades of blue or black are not.

2. Nervousness

Let's face it, you are going to be nervous. I was nervous at my first interview…and my second…and my third—and you will be, too. But whomever you interview with will also know that you are nervous—they certainly went through many interviews themselves and know exactly what those butterflies in their stomachs mean. This will not be a new experience for them, and they will be well aware that you bring a level of nervousness into any interview situation.

Nervousness can be manifested in several ways:

- Sweaty palms

- An upset stomach

- A dry mouth

- An increased heartbeat

- Goosebumps

- Trembling knees

- Twitching eyebrows

- Increased rate of breathing

Please keep in mind that these are *natural* psychological and physiological reactions to stress. Early humans experienced these same feelings whenever they came face to face with a saber-toothed tiger or an opponent with a bigger rock to throw. Humans down through the ages have always experienced bouts of nervousness whenever faced with a situation outside their "comfort zone"—a situation that was not normally part of their daily activities. And interviews certainly qualify in that regard.

But let's allow that nervousness to work to your advantage! In a stressful situation, like an interview, your body is releasing larger amounts of adrenalin than it normally does (thus all the physical manifestations mentioned above). Interestingly, this increased level of nervousness is advantageous because it will help keep you focused more than if you were overconfident and/or complacent. It is your body's way of telling you that you need to be ready for the task before you. It's not a normal event; it's an event that requires your absolute attention, complete concentration, and due diligence.

Here are some important points to keep in mind:

- The key to managing your nervousness is preparation. If you researched the school, practiced appropriate interview questions (and your responses), and considered various interview types, and if you are aware of the common mistakes teacher candidates often make, know the key principles for interview success, and know the questions you should ask—in other words, if you read (several times) and practiced all the chapters in this book—you will have the confidence you need to *ace your teacher interview*.

- Remember, you are in control. In fact, you are in control of much of the interview situation. You determine when you are going to arrive at the interview, what clothes you are going to wear, how you are going to sit, how prepared you are going to be to answer typical interview questions, what questions you are going to pose to the interviewer, and what level of confidence you are going to display during the interview. You are in control of many interview factors that can have a significant, positive effect on the success of that interview.

INSIDER TIP

One of my students made it a point to make the following chant a part of her mental preparation (she practiced yoga) in the week leading up to her first interview: "I am in control, I am in control, I am in control." She would say it over and over to herself in the shower, while driving to student teaching, while shopping, and just before she went to bed. She discovered that she was considerably less nervous when meeting the principal than she had ever anticipated.

- Consider that each interview is a practice session for the next one. The more interviews you engage in, the better prepared you will be for any succeeding interviews. Each interview will teach you something new, providing you with more confidence and self-assurance for subsequent interviews. That's why it is always important to go through a personal checklist of self-evaluative questions immediately after every interview (see Appendix B). It would be equally important to go through several practice or mock interviews with college professors, area administrators willing to provide that service, family members, or local businesspeople.

Keep in mind that nervousness is normal. The key is to be in control of your nervousness, rather than having the nervousness control you.

3. Enthusiasm

The reasons you want to be a teacher are undoubtedly many. Who you are as a person and how you would like to share your personality with students are significant factors in why you chose to be a teacher. So, too, will they be significant in terms of your success in an interview. A teacher's personality is a major and predominant factor in the success of students within that teacher's influence as well as the success that teacher will experience in an interview situation.

Good classroom teachers are joyful. They are excited about learning, and they transmit that excitement to their students. They relish in the thrill of discovery and the natural curiosity of students. And they are stimulated by the unknown and are amazed at what *can* be learned, not just at what *is* learned.

Those three factors—who you are, your personality, and your excitement about teaching—should also be part of any teacher interview. You must demonstrate your *passion* for teaching! If you are passionate about teaching, it will come through loud and clear in an interview. On the other hand, if you are noncommittal, blasé, or simply "flat," that will also show up. Your passion for teaching must be evident in every word you say, question you answer, and gesture you use.

There are three major components every interviewer looks for in a potential employee: expertise, trustworthiness, and dynamism. Dynamism means that you must be "energized" about teaching and kids—that teaching is your *raison d'être*. This sense of dynamism, which you show through your excitement and enthusiasm, means that nothing will stop you from providing a group of students with learning opportunities second to none and that you have a positive personality, a sunny disposition, and a friendly demeanor. You are a doer, not a watcher. You are an advocate, not a complainer. And you are an explorer, not a "paper pusher."

You must exude enthusiasm for teaching in what you say and how you say it. Obviously, you don't want to go overboard, but you do want to let the interviewer know of your excitement and enthusiasm. You do want to demonstrate your *passion*.

4. Body Language

Body language is a significant source of information about an individual. It consists of body posture, hand and facial gestures, and facial expressions. Although there is much still to be learned about the effect of body language on how we perceive others, we do know that as much as 70 percent of human communication consists of body language—with the remainder consisting of words themselves.

The body language you display in a teacher interview will provide the interviewer with important clues about your attitude or your state of mind. For example, how you present yourself may indicate traits such as aggressiveness, boredom, amusement, pleasure, relaxation, lack of interest, dishonesty, or fear. In short, the position of your body (and body parts) during an interview will have a significant bearing on how you will be perceived as a person and as a teacher.

Here are some tips on how you can present yourself in the best way:

- Please practice your handshake. This is a critical "first impression"; the quality of your handshake can frequently determine how well the interview begins. A good handshake (for both men and women) should not be too limp (denotes insecurity, disinterest, and weakness) or too firm (denotes aggression, control, and overt authority). Here are a few tips for the ideal handshake:
  - Look the person in the eye (don't look at the hands doing the shaking).
  - Lean slightly in toward the person with your right shoulder.
  - Extend your right arm so that it is parallel with the floor.
  - Grasp the right hand of the other person with the thumbs interlocked.
  - As soon as your hands touch, make a verbal greeting ("Good morning, Mr. Jensen. It's a pleasure to meet you.").
  - Give the other person's hand a single firm shake, up and down about one or two inches.

- Make sure you give the other person the same amount of hand pressure as he or she is giving you.

- Let go. Don't hang on too long.

I know it probably seems silly and old-fashioned, but the quality of a handshake (and an accompanying smile) is the first vital piece of information an interviewer learns about you. Give a sloppy handshake, a limp handshake, or a "muscle-shake" and you may send the wrong message even before the interview actually begins. I *strongly suggest* several practice sessions with adults (not fellow students). A handshake may seem like a minor element of an interview; but it has major implications.

INSIDER TIP

Oh, my gosh! Do I even need to mention it? PLEASE—no "fist bumps"!

- When sitting down, don't hunch your shoulders. Try to sit with your shoulders squared and your back straight.

- Never fold your arms across your chest. This is often seen as a sign of aggression or superiority—these are not good traits.

- Occasionally nod your head as the interviewer talks with you. This shows your interest without interrupting the flow of conversation. However, don't turn into a bobble-head; keep the nodding to an acceptable level.

- Make sure your head is erect. Don't tip it to the side. Try to focus on keeping your chin parallel to the floor. When in doubt, always try to keep your eyes focused on the bridge of the interviewer's nose.

- When sitting down, keep your feet close together or cross your legs. A wide space between your feet or knees is often interpreted as a signal that you are bored or uncommitted. Also, don't swing your legs back and forth, tap your foot on the floor, bounce your leg up and down, slide your feet in and out of your shoes, or continually cross and uncross your legs.

- Be aware of your facial expressions. Our facial expressions can cause physiological reactions in our bodies. For example, if our face is screwed up tight, we feel anxious. On the other hand, if we relax our facial muscles, our entire body relaxes, too. Other negative facial expressions include tight lips, squinted eyes, and frowns. You should practice with pleasant and relaxed facial expressions. The best one of all: a smile...an honest, sincere, and personable smile. Remember what Victor Borge once said, "A smile is the shortest distance between two people." That's great advice for an interview, too.

- Occasionally, use hand gestures to make a point or to emphasize your enthusiasm. Don't overdo it, however. On the other hand, there are some hand gestures you should never do. Here's a list of some of the most annoying or distracting:
  - Cracking your knuckles
  - Scratching yourself
  - Tapping a pen or pencil
  - Touching or smoothing your hair
  - Putting your hand or fingers in front of your mouth
  - Stroking your chin
  - Biting your nails
  - Jiggling keys or coins in your pocket
  - Bending a paper clip back and forth
  - Touching your face
  - Folding your hands behind your head
  - Fixing or smoothing your clothing
  - Twisting your ring around on your finger

The best advice: Fold your hands on your lap or hold a pen in one hand (please don't click it or tap it) and a notebook or legal pad in the other.

Lean slightly into the interview. A slight lean conveys your interest in the interviewer and in the interview. Don't overdo this, however. The lean should be almost imperceptible, the top half of your back slightly away from the chair back and the bottom half of your back against the chair back. This posture is a good one to practice well before the interview.

FROM THE PRINCIPAL'S DESK:

"I also like to see how the body responds under pressure. The body language at the interview will give me insight as to what I can expect in the future."

5. *Body Parts and Adornment*

- **Men:** Shave your face the morning of the interview. If you wear a beard or mustache, please make sure it's trimmed neatly within 24 hours of the interview. Get a haircut a few days in advance of a scheduled interview. And, please, trim your nose hairs.

- **Women:** Style your hair conservatively; no fancy hairdos and no purple or pink streaks. Go very lightly on any perfume—again, you want them to remember *you*, not how you smelled.

- **Men and Women:** I know this seems like silly advice, but please use a deodorant. I once interviewed a candidate who didn't, and I couldn't wait until he got out of the room, out of the school, and out of town.

INSIDER TIP

Interestingly, some recent research suggests a link between how one smells and personality. For example, if you want to make a good (olfactory) impression, smell like pure simple soap because people often associate cleanliness with confidence and success.

- If you have eyebrow rings, nose studs, tongue rings, tapers, tunnels, plugs, spirals, or other metal objects in your face or body, please remove them. If you frequently wear 17 earrings in your left ear and 9 in your right ear, you might want to consider removing them, too.

- If you have any visible tattoos, think about how you can remove them from view. This may involve wearing a long sleeve shirt or blouse to cover a tattoo on your arm, a wide bracelet to hide a tattoo on your wrist, or dark stockings to cover a tattoo on your ankle. I recently had a student who had some extremely elaborate tattoos from his neck all the way down to his ankles. As he prepared for his first interview, he knew he would have to wear a high collar shirt and cover his feet with long dark socks. He succeeded brilliantly and nobody knew about his body art. (As a follow-up, it should be mentioned that he now teaches middle school. Because he always wears long-sleeved shirts, not even his students know about the dragons and wizards adorning his torso.)

- Cut and/or trim your fingernails. Clean them too. (If you have dirty fingernails, I certainly don't want to be shaking your hand.)

6. Eye Contact

In the United States, if you have good eye contact with a person, it generally means you are interested in the person and in what that person is saying. On the other hand, if you look down or away from a person rather than meeting his or her gaze, you are considered to be uninterested or unconcerned. It is frequently a signal that you lack sufficient self-confidence.

In other countries around the world, eye contact has different connotations. In some Middle Eastern cultures, eye contact is considered to be inappropriate in accordance with religious laws. In several African countries, extended eye contact is taken as a challenge of authority. In some Asian cultures, lack of eye contact is a sign of respect. However, in a job interview situation (in North America, at least), eye contact between a candidate and an interviewer conveys trustworthiness, honesty, and interest—three qualities you want a potential employer to know about you.

When you answer questions in an interview, always look directly at the person asking the question. If you are in a group or panel interview, address the specific person asking the question rather than the entire panel. If you ask a question, don't look down or to the side; rather, look directly at the individual and pose your question to a specific individual.

> ✔**EXTRA CREDIT**
>
> Good eye contact helps establish a good rapport between the interviewer and you. Just as important, it helps to signal your interest in the conversation and your desire to accurately and effectively answer each and every question.

If eye contact if difficult for you, you may wish to conduct some mock interviews with family members or friends. Practice looking directly into a person's eyes as you talk and answer questions. You may even wish to practice by placing a chair in front of a full-length mirror and having a conversation with yourself.

It's vitally important that you practice this nonverbal behavior. If you appear to be "shifty-eyed" or indirect in responding to questions, an interviewer may get the impression that you are less than forthright in your responses or are trying to hide something. Those are certainly not impressions you want to leave with any potential employer.

7. Voice

It's not always what you say, but how you say it that leaves an impression with the interviewer. This would be a good time to go back and review the notes you recorded in the "Introduction to Speech" course you took in your freshman year. It would also be a good time to practice appropriate speech patterns that will help put you in the most favorable light.

Here are a few tips to keep in mind:

- Make sure you can project your voice at a level that can be heard five or six feet away (the average distance between interviewee and interviewer). If you tend to speak softly, I would suggest several practice sessions or mock interviews so you can practice projecting.

- Always be sure you articulate your words and your responses. While you will undoubtedly want to practice some of the questioning scenarios included in this book, you shouldn't get so comfortable with them that you get lazy in accurately pronouncing the words, phrases, and sentences. Typically, when you are nervous (as in an interview), you have a tendency to hurry through the pronunciation of words. You may want to consider slowing down your speech a little as you respond to a question.

- Use correct grammar. I remember one student who would use the word "like" constantly in her speech ("It was, like, you know, like, the time when the teacher, like, was telling the kids, like, they should, like, settle down. It was, like, difficult for us to, like, get them back on task."). You may want to ask an older adult to listen to you to see if there are any grammatical habits that need attention.

- Pace yourself. Again, when we are nervous we tend to talk faster than we want to and faster than someone can understand us. Make yourself a mental note to speak a little slower than you would to your friends or classmates.

- It's always a good idea to pause every so often when responding to a question. Pausing puts extra emphasis on a particular point ("When I visited Franklin High School last month, [pause] I was really taken by the high level of student energy and enthusiasm in the hallways!"). It is also appropriate to pause briefly before responding to a question. If you answer too quickly, it may send a signal that you're answering with the first thing that pops into your head. On the other hand, when you pause briefly before you answer, it demonstrates that you are carefully considering the question as well as the most appropriate reply. Thoughtful responses always get you more points than do quick responses.

- Vary your tone of voice. Try not to speak in a monotone or in a "flat" voice. Occasionally add some inflection or change your tone of voice to demonstrate your enthusiasm, motivation, and interest. If you want to appear interested in the position, one sure suggestion is to add some honest inflections into your responses. You may say you are interested in becoming a teacher at Sunnydale Middle School, but it will be your tone of voice—rather than just your words—that will convey that interest most directly.

Using the Essential Seven

Nonverbal behaviors can make a big difference, more than the responses to formal interview questions. Taking the time—ahead of any interview—to practice and assess your nonverbal behaviors can help you reap multiple "brownie points" during the course of any interview. Please don't neglect this all-important and critical element of any successful interview.

CHAPTER 6

THE SINGLE-MOST IMPORTANT QUESTION YOU MUST ALWAYS ANSWER!

It's the one question that is always in the mind of any interviewer. It doesn't matter whether you are interviewing for a job flipping burgers at your local fast-food restaurant, for the CEO position at a major company, or for a position as the manager of a minor league baseball club—every interviewer has this question on his or her mind. And here's why it is important—the question will never be asked in any interview, but it must always be answered.

The question is this:

#1: How will this person make my job easier?

You are being interviewed because the interviewer hopes you can bring value, dedication, and expertise to the job. Those qualities are what any boss wants to see in his or her employees. Those qualities help the boss (principal) do his or her job better and ensure that a product (education) gets into the hands of the consumer (students). That single question will never come up in any interview, but if you can answer the question—several times during the interview—you will put yourself heads and shoulders above the rest of the competition and ensure a very favorable assessment on the interview.

For most bosses—and for every building principal—their responsibilities are numerous and non-stop. They must handle a whirlwind of responsibilities, demands, schedules, unexpected events, and last-minute chores that strain their patience and their resolve. It's like a circus performer who juggles 15 bowling balls while encouraging a dozen lions to jump through flaming hoops, all while walking a tightrope a hundred feet in the air. And that's every day. To say that principals are overworked and overscheduled would be to understate the obvious.

Each of those principals is looking for ways to maximize his or her performance and minimize stress. If you can demonstrate ways in which you will make the principal's job a little easier—a little less crazy and a little less stressful—then you will be the one he or she remembers when it comes time to make a final decision on who gets hired and who doesn't.

INSIDER TIP

An interview is like a sales pitch. You are trying to sell a product, and the interviewer wants to purchase the best product available. Only in this case you are not trying to sell "you." Rather, you are trying to sell the benefits of you. How will you benefit the school?

Here's an example:

Josh was interviewing for a third-grade position at Shady Lane Elementary School. A week before the interview, he read an article in the local newspaper about how the school's reading scores were going down. During the interview the principal asked him, "What will you be able to bring to this position?"

Josh responded, "During my student teaching experience I worked with another teacher in setting up an after-school tutoring program for students who were below grade level in reading. We met with the kids twice a week and offered them one-on-one tutoring services in addition to an outreach program for parents on how they can get actively involved in their children's reading growth and development. By the end of the tenth week, the kids were showing reading gains of 27 to 39 percent.

"I would like to have the opportunity to initiate a similar venture here—giving kids an extra chance in reading and working closely with their parents to promote reading in a very positive way. I believe my experience and organizational skills can go a long way in helping the program be successful."

By reading the article, Josh knew that the school was experiencing some challenges in regard to students' growth and development in reading. He also surmised (correctly) that this was a concern of the principal, simply because it had been featured in the local paper. So Josh wisely decided to address the principal's concern and answer the question that was in the back of her mind, the question she never asked: How will this person make my job easier?

FROM THE PRINCIPAL'S DESK:

"The two best pieces of interview advice I can offer teacher candidates are 1) Research the district prior to the interview, and 2) Share how they will be a team player."

Here's how another candidate answered the question:

> Heather wanted to teach more than anything else in the world. She also knew that the competition for the 10th-grade social studies position at Central High School was fierce. Six students from her college were applying for that position in addition to dozens of others from various colleges and universities. The principal, Mr. Grove, had a tough choice to make.
>
> During the course of the interview, Mr. Grove made two or three references to the school newspaper; it had gone through four different student editors since the start of the year and the morale among the staff was low. Heather sensed his concern and in response to the question "What would you say is your greatest strength?" Heather replied, "I'm a goal-oriented person. My greatest strength is my ability to *be* organized and *stay* organized. My classroom and my lesson plans are always well-planned and in order. For example, I believe I can bring those organizational skills to the school newspaper. I worked for two years on the college newspaper before my student teaching semester. I've taken a few journalism courses and interned at our local newspaper one summer—my uncle is the managing editor—where I worked in a number of departments. I enjoy a challenge and would welcome the opportunity to bring my background of experiences with journalism and newspapers to Central High School. If assigned as a faculty advisor, I can assure you of a newspaper operation that will be successful—and very organized."

Notice how Heather quickly surmised that the operation of the school newspaper was an ongoing concern of the principal. She quickly looked for an opportunity to share how her unique experiences and qualifications might help the principal—to make his job just a little easier.

As you might guess, the key to answering this never-asked question is to be prepared before the interview and to listen carefully for clues during the interview when you can provide several responses to the query. Every principal has challenges that he or she must meet. If you can show how you can assist in that process, then you will be establishing yourself as a candidate any principal would love to have on the staff.

✔**EXTRA CREDIT**

By visiting the school ahead of time, checking out the school or district Web site, and talking with teachers, students, or parents in the local community, you can obtain some very valuable information that will help you formulate appropriate answers during the course of the interview.

Here's how Tyler responded to the unasked question during the course of his interview with Mr. Hamilton at First Street Elementary School:

Mr. Hamilton:	In reviewing your resume, I noticed that you've spent quite a bit of time with a group called Camp Wildcat. Can you tell me what that is?
Tyler:	Certainly. It's a student organization at the University of Arizona that works with underprivileged students from throughout Tucson. We offer several camping experiences throughout the year at a facility several miles outside of town. University students volunteer as counselors, activity leaders, tutors, cooks, and a whole variety of other jobs. It's a way of offering kids outdoor activities and experiences they may not get in an urban environment.
Mr. Hamilton:	What kinds of things did you do?
Tyler:	When I first got to the U of A, I heard about this group during student orientation. I knew I wanted to get involved, because I was planning to be a teacher. I started working in the student office and then volunteered for some of the weekend camps. I was hooked! I ran for Assistant Camp Director and was elected in my junior year. I was put in charge of organizing the summer camp program, recruiting student volunteers, and coordinating all the activities—all while taking a full load of classes. Because I'm a detail person, I was able to stay focused and organized while still maintaining my sanity. I love working with people—particularly when we all have the same goal in mind. It was a very successful venture, and I believe I was able to use my talents in a very positive way—helping less-fortunate kids grow and learn.

Through his response, Tyler gave Mr. Hamilton information he needed, but never asked for. Tyler demonstrated that he was organized, goal-oriented, a team player, and someone who always has kids' best interests in mind. These are all qualities of great teachers that principals want in their teaching staff. Tyler was never asked if he had those qualities, but he took the time to answer the unasked question.

During the course of an interview, you can create one or more "openings" that will provide you with opportunities to respond to this never-asked question. Notice how Jennifer set up (in a very positive way) Mrs. Morrison, the principal at Red Ridge Elementary School:

Mrs. Morrison:	Well, it's been a very interesting conversation, Jennifer. We've talked about many things. Are there any questions you'd like to ask?
Jennifer:	Yes. Given the current emphasis on inquiry-based science, I'm wondering what challenges your teachers are having in meeting the demands of an inquiry-based curriculum?
Mrs. Morrison:	We have several older teachers who haven't had a lot of training on inquiry-based science. They've found it to be a real struggle in designing lesson plans that are more student-centered and less teacher-directed.
Jennifer:	Well, science is one of my passions. In our science methods course, we learned how to write inquiry-based lesson plans. During my student teaching experience I had the opportunity to help other fourth-grade teachers craft lesson plans using an inquiry model. I also worked with my major professor on a project to bring more inquiry-based science into some local schools.
Mrs. Morrison:	It sounds like you have a real passion for inquiry-based science.
Jennifer:	Yes, I do. I'd like to bring that passion here to Red Ridge. I believe I have the skills and energy that can re-invigorate the overall science program. I'm a good organizer, I work very well with people, and I love writing science units. I'd welcome the opportunity to work with Red Ridge teachers on designing and implementing a new science curriculum. I love challenges, and I love hard work!

Jennifer gave Mrs. Morrison an opportunity to share one of the school's ongoing struggles. Then Jennifer provided a response that highlighted one of her strengths as well as her willingness to address that challenge. Mrs. Morrison never asked Jennifer, "How will this person make my job easier?" but Jennifer took the time to answer the question and, not surprisingly, secure the job.

CHAPTER 7

123 BASIC INTERVIEW QUESTIONS (AND 123 FANTASTIC RESPONSES)

The 123 questions that follow are those most frequently asked at any teacher interview. By reading over these questions—several times—you will be well-prepared to respond when they are asked at your own interview. By practicing the answers to these questions—again, several times—you will be equally well-prepared to impress a principal or administrator posing the questions. Feel comfortable with these questions and answers, and you will not only stand out from the rest of the crowd, you will provide the interviewer with valuable information necessary to securing the position.

Of course, you won't hear every question in this section of the book (simply because most interviews last between 30 and 45 minutes—or from 10 to 20 questions). Quite possibly, you may hear different variations of these questions. The key is to become so familiar with these queries that you will be able to successfully respond to all of them no matter which ones are asked, how they are asked, or how they may be modified.

INSIDER TIP

Don't memorize the responses as they are written in this book. Make these answers your own. Infuse them with your own unique personality and your own unique experiences as a teacher candidate. In other words, let "you" shine through.

Remember, the interviewer is not interested in stock answers to these questions; instead, he or she wants the opportunity to experience the individual behind the resume, the GPA, and the application for employment. He or she wants to hire a person, not someone who memorized all the answers in *Ace Your Teacher Interview*.

If you took a writing course in college, you may recall the maxim "Show, don't tell!" In other words, if you are writing a fictional story about Mrs. Foster, a frustrated housewife, don't *tell* your reader that Mrs. Foster is angry (for example); *show* how she is angry because she throws dinner plates around the kitchen, screams at the cat, kicks over the trashcan, and tosses a bowl of spaghetti at her husband. The same advice holds true for an interview. That is, don't *tell* an interviewer, "I like working with children." Instead, *show* the interviewer how you like children: "During my student teaching experience, I worked with my cooperating teacher to set up an after-school soccer program for the kids in the public housing project on the south side of town." Don't just *tell* the interviewer about yourself; *show* the interviewer what you have done and what you can do.

It's also a good idea to practice filling your responses with facts ("During my tenure as vice-president of the Student Education Association, we were able to increase attendance by 64 percent in one year.") rather than with generalities ("I'm a people person."). It's equally important that you share information that sets you apart from the competition and allows the interviewer to know who you are as an individual. "I like to teach science" is a general response almost anyone can say. However, "I was able to get my students involved in a four-week Butterfly Discovery Project at the City Center Museum, and it really changed their attitudes about science" provides specific information about you—and nobody else!

I invite you to read through the sample questions and responses in this section. Read this part of the book several times and become comfortable with all the typical teacher interview questions—many of which you will be asked. After several readings, I would invite you to begin crafting your own unique responses using the suggestions and ideas shared with each of these queries. You may wish to make an audio recording of the questions and practice (in front of a mirror, for example) your individual response to each one. You will discover that the more you practice, the more comfortable you will be. Your comfort in answering these questions will go a long way in helping you secure the teaching position you want.

A. General Questions

#2:   What do you know about this school?

A: According to the school's Web page, you have achieved AYP in each of the past five years. Your reading scores are up, and your math scores are making some significant improvements. That says to me that your teachers are sincerely committed to integrating some instructional changes to the reading and math curricula. Along with the two extra days of in-service training recently approved by the school board, this underscores a sincere commitment to the needs of students. I've talked with several teachers and—to a person—they are all impressed, and all supportive of, the new schedule. This schedule makes additional time available for literacy instruction—something that is showing up in the improvement of test scores. Some of the parents have even remarked on a new sense of energy in the school—certainly something to be proud of.

This is a frequent question in any interview. Simply put, the interviewer wants to know if you've done your homework. What do you know about the school other than how many teachers work there and the color of the hallways? Make sure you take the time to pour over school board minutes, the school's Web site, and any printed newsletters or brochures. Talk with people in the school—teachers, maintenance staff, bus drivers—and learn as much as you can about the climate and philosophy. Chat with parents and community members in the supermarket, hardware store, or gas station. Learn anything you can, and plan to share that knowledge in the interview.

> ✔**EXTRA CREDIT**
>
> You can always get extra points if you research the school's recent test scores and frame some sort of positive comment around those scores. For example, "I see that you've made an 8 percent improvement in your reading scores over last year. You must be very proud." Or, "I note that your recent math scores have held firm over the last three years. I'd like to contribute my enthusiasm and expertise in teaching math in helping to improve those results."

———————————

#3:   Why do you want to teach in this school/district?

A: When I visited in February, I had the opportunity to talk with some teachers about your new writing program. When I checked out the school's Web site and saw how much writing was integrated throughout the curriculum, I became even more excited. I really believe that writing can enhance the middle school program, and, with my writing background, I can make a positive contribution to that effort. I like the emphasis on writing, and I like the opportunities for contributing to that effort.

This is a golden opportunity to demonstrate all the homework you did on the school or district (see Chapter 2). Your response should make it clear that you know something about this specific school or district as well as how you can contribute to their overall academic effort. Here's where you can "stroke their feathers" and tell them what a good job they are doing.

#4:   What are the essential traits of an effective educator?

A: I believe that good teachers are effective because they assume five interrelated roles. One, they serve as positive role models for their students. They model their excitement and enthusiasm for a topic consistently and daily. Two, effective educators are student oriented. They truly care for their students, and they exhibit empathy—trying to see the world through their students' eyes. Third, effective teachers are task oriented. They concentrate on the instructional activities that cause learning to happen rather than on procedures. Fourth, they are good classroom managers. They understand that classroom management is not about achieving order for order's sake; it's about achieving order so productive learning can occur. And, fifth, good teachers are lifelong learners. They continually add to their knowledge base throughout their teaching careers. I strongly believe in these principles and plan to make them part of my teaching repertoire throughout my career.

This is an excellent question, and your response should demonstrate your knowledge of what good teachers do as well as how you plan to embrace those principles. This is the time to show that you know your research and what that research means in terms of your own teaching career.

#5:   What gives you the greatest pleasure in teaching?

A: I call it the "light bulb effect." It's that time in a lesson, unit, or discussion when a student "gets it"—when that proverbial light bulb goes off over his or her head. There's nothing like it in the world! It's when that look of recognition crosses a student's face, when a student exclaims, "Hey, this is really cool!" or jumps up and down with unmitigated excitement. There's a joy in the discovery and an enthusiasm in the voice as students realize that they now understand something they didn't previously. That's what I want to work for with all my students. I want them all to experience that "light bulb effect" in each and every subject throughout the school year.

Your answer should underscore your reasons for becoming a teacher. Your response should be a validation of why you decided to enter this profession and what you will do in order to be one of the best. Most important, there should be passion in your response!

#6:   What kind of principal would you like to work for?

A: From my own observations and conversations with teachers, I think that a good relationship with a building principal needs to be based on trust and communication. I can certainly help in that regard by always keeping my principal informed. I know that the last thing any administrator needs or wants is a surprise. If I was inviting a guest speaker into my classroom, setting up a terrarium with a collection of snakes, or assigning a controversial book for my students to read, I would want to inform my principal. I've learned that keeping the principal in the loop, information-wise, is always a good idea. If I have a problem student or anticipate the storming of the office by an irate parent, I should let my principal know early on. A well-informed principal can assist me in working through a problem, particularly if he or she has information early in the process. That information sharing is critical in establishing trust and open lines of communication between me and my principal.

If you go back to Chapter 6, you'll note that your answer to this question is also an answer to the single-most important question. Administrators want to hire people who will not create problems, but will make the principal's job a little easier. You will note that a good response to this query is proactive rather than reactive. Rather than describe the principal (which may or may not match the person interviewing you), explain what you will do to enhance a positive teacher/principal relationship. You'll get more points that way.

INSIDER TIP

Some books recommend that you take notes throughout the interview. My conversations with principals reveal that it's a bad idea simply because it's difficult to write, listen, and develop a rapport all at the same time. You are frequently distracted and often mis-focused. My advice: Save the multi-tasking for another time.

#7:   **How would you describe the ideal teacher?**

A: The ideal teacher is someone who embraces and practices several standards of good teaching. I believe that three are critical and necessary for good teaching to take place. First, the ideal teacher understands how children learn and can develop learning opportunities that support their intellectual, social, and personal development. Second, the ideal teacher uses an understanding of individual and group motivation and behavior to create a learning environment that encourages positive social interaction, active engagement in learning, and self motivation. And, third, the ideal teacher understands and uses formal and informal assessment strategies that ensure the continuous intellectual development of all learners. While these are certainly not the only standards good teachers should practice, I believe them to be three of the most important.

This is a question you're likely to be asked near the beginning of the interview. Then the interviewer will try to determine (throughout the remainder of the interview) if, indeed, you are the candidate who best exemplifies these ideals. It's equally important that you know what good teachers do (and how you would embrace that philosophy) in response to those concepts.

FROM THE PRINCIPAL'S DESK:

"Last spring we had an interview with a candidate who was so passionate about students and helping them in any way she could that she made all of us cry."

#8:   **What is the most important quality of a teacher?**

A: In my discussions with teachers during my field experiences and at the school where I student taught, I believe that the number one characteristic of a good teacher is flexibility or the ability to roll with the punches and not let the little things get you down. I realize that there is no such thing as an average day in teaching. Machines break down, lessons don't work, technology goes on the blink, students get sick, and a hundred other things can, and often do, go wrong. But it's the flexible teacher—the one who doesn't let these inevitable events get in his or her way—who survives and teaches best. I suppose it's the inflexible teachers who burn out and leave the profession.

As with the previous question, this one will be presented early in the interview process. Have your answer ready; but, more important, have several examples or anecdotes you can share later in the interview that will support your response. Demonstrate that you not only know what good teachers do, but that you've had experiences that make you one of those outstanding educators.

#9:   What skills do you think are most critical to this position?

A: For me, three basic skills stand out: 1) The ability to effectively manage student behavior; to create a classroom structure that both supports students and helps them succeed in an environment with high expectations and individual attention. 2) Time management—being able to effectively manage all the duties and responsibilities of classroom teaching in a productive and efficient way. And 3) Creating a "community of learners" that celebrates learning and success for every child; a classroom environment in which everyone works together for a common purpose. I know these are tough challenges for any beginning teacher, but I believe I have the persistence and experience to make them happen.

Again, as in so many of the questions you might be asked about yourself, be very specific and offer detailed information about your goals and how you will make them happen. Don't be wishy-washy, but don't be over-confident either. Tap into some of your student teaching experiences, and offer the interviewer some concrete examples of how you took advantage of your skills.

#10:   Why did you apply for this position?

A: Dinosaur Elementary School has an excellent reputation in the community. According to your Web page, your overall reading test scores are up significantly—and your math scores in third and fifth grades show significant improvement over last year. You obviously have a committed staff, and I like to be part of a winning team. You also have a dynamic staff-development program for teachers. In my conversations with some of the teachers, they remarked on the variety of workshops that have been offered that were geared for their specific needs. While the emphasis has been on reading instruction, there have been sessions devoted to math and science as well. I believe every teacher, no matter what their experience, can profit from additional training. That's something else that has also impressed me about Dinosaur.

This is an opportunity for you to highlight your special knowledge about the school or district. It signals to the interviewer that you took the time to do your homework, learning specific details other candidates may not have investigated.

#11:   What does it mean to be a successful teacher?

A: I believe successful teachers have five distinctive qualities that set them apart from the so-called "average teacher." For me, a successful teacher is flexible, someone who can take charge no matter what the situation or circumstances. Second, I think successful teachers must exhibit a sense of fairness throughout the classroom, treating all students equally in the same situation. Third, all outstanding teachers have high expectations for each and every one of their students. Fourth, and this is absolutely critical, successful teachers have a consistently positive attitude. They don't let the little things get them down, and they serve as positive role models for their students. Finally, the most successful teachers have a sense of humor. Not cracking jokes all the time, but rather looking at the bright side of things, laughing out loud, and using self-deprecating humor when appropriate. As elements of successful teachers, those items are also personal goals for me as I begin this lifelong journey.

This is another question designed to tap into your personal philosophy. It is strongly suggested that you respond in the first person rather than in the more distant third person. Let the interviewer know that you are, or you have the potential to become, a successful teacher.

> **✔EXTRA CREDIT**
> Every response should be colored with some degree of enthusiasm. After all, they want to hire a person, not an emotionless resume.

#12:   What do you think is wrong with education today?

A: I actually believe there's a lot going right with education today. Teachers are more involved in efforts to improve the literacy levels of their students. School boards are wrestling with money issues, but they are also deeply committed to ensuring that the resources necessary for good teaching to take place are available. Schools are focused on helping more students be successful in mathematics, with improved textbooks and more manipulatives. Teachers are taking an active role in curriculum development, ensuring a sense of ownership in the educational process. And there is a wave of eager, excited, and well-trained new teachers coming into the field— new teachers with an enthusiasm about education, a deep commitment to students, and a willingness to work as members of a committed team. Sure, there are challenges, but I'd prefer to look at the teaching glass as half-full rather than half-empty.

Some interviewers use this as a "trick" question. Be careful! Basically, the interviewer wants a sense of how you view the world in general and how you view education specifically. Don't make the mistake of focusing on the negative, but rather share some positive and personal perspectives on what you see to be right. This is also a great opportunity to show how your training and attitude can make a difference in the education of young people.

B. Questions About You

#13:   **What is your greatest strength as a teacher?**

A: I believe I have three primary strengths which I would like to bring to Prairie Pines Elementary School. First, I am well-versed in all the aspects of reading instruction. I took extra reading courses as an undergraduate and worked closely with my advisor in the college reading clinic. Second, I'm a team player. I enjoy working with people. My work as a student ambassador, a member of the student senate, and as an R.A. in one of the dorms have given me many opportunities to work with people. Third, I enjoy learning. I spend a lot of time reading professional magazines and was able to attend two education conferences in my senior year. I hope to bring my passion for learning to a classroom at Prairie Pines.

This is a great opportunity to "sell" yourself. Even though the question asks for "your greatest strength," you should consider a response that outlines two or three strengths. This gives the interviewer a more complete picture of who you are. Most important: This is the time to be confident, not arrogant. Be honest, but don't pontificate. Provide specific details, but don't spend a lot of time patting yourself on the back.

#14:   What is your philosophy of teaching?

A: I believe teachers act as facilitators of the learning process rather than
monitors. When we sincerely invite youngsters to select and direct their
own learning experiences (and teach them to do just that), they can achieve
a measure of independence and motivation that will carry them beyond the
classroom. The way we teach is as important as—if not more important
than—what we teach. Indeed, the chief role of a competent educator is to
guide students in their own explorations, providing them with the tools they
need and the necessary instruction to use those tools and then giving them
the chance to discover the joys and excitement of learning as a personal goal
rather than a dictated one.

Before any interview, write out your personal philosophy of teaching. If it's not
included as part of the job application form, it will certainly be included as part of
the interview. Being able to express your personal philosophy at the drop of a hat is
critical and will provide you with a solid foundation for a successful interview.

#15:   Describe your teaching style.

A: Several studies have helped us look at the teaching-learning partnership
in a new way. Researchers have discovered, for example, that learning is
not simply the accumulation of knowledge (which is passive), but rather
how we make sense of knowledge. This is constructivism, and my teaching
style is constructivist. I know that knowledge is created in the mind of the
learner and that I need to help students relate new content to the knowledge
they already have. I also need to provide students with opportunities to
process and apply that knowledge in meaningful situations, what one of my
professors called a "hands-on, minds-on" approach to learning. Some of the
ways I practice constructivism in the classroom include linking background
knowledge with textual knowledge, asking lots of open-ended questions,
assisting children in pursuing answers to their self-initiated queries,
engaging students in metacognitive thinking, and promoting self-initiated
investigations and discoveries. I believe that the most important lesson I can
teach youngsters is that knowledge is never a product; rather, it is a process.

Show that you are up to date on the latest educational practices and designs.
Demonstrate how that knowledge has become part of who you are or what you do
in a classroom environment. What do you believe, and why do you believe it?

#16:   What two things would you like to improve about yourself?

A: The two things I would like to improve on over the next few years are my computer skills and my time-management skills. I'm currently addressing my computer skills in a course I plan to take this summer at Prestigious University. While I can effectively integrate technology into all my subject areas, the field is changing so rapidly that I should make sure I'm getting the latest information. It's a process I plan to continue throughout my teaching career. I'd also like to improve my time management. I tend to be one of those people who always tries to do too much. I often find that there are not enough hours in the day to get everything accomplished. I need to prioritize my work better and give myself some time for reflection and inquiry.

Interviewers often ask this question in order to find out about some of your weaknesses. It's always a good idea to respond with "deficits" that everyone wrestles with. Things like time management, patience, technological skills, and attitude are items we all could improve. The best answer for this question is one that focuses on "improvements" related directly to teaching. In other words, don't tell the interviewer that you'd like to improve the quality of the beverages at your Friday night poker game or that you'd like to find more time to update your *Facebook* account this week.

INSIDER TIP

Whenever you can, demonstrate that you are mature enough to handle constructive criticism.

#17:   What book are you currently reading or have you read recently?

A: I think that teachers of reading should also be readers themselves. That's always a good model for kids. In my "Introduction to American Education" course during my sophomore year, I was introduced to Jonathan Kozol. I'm now re-reading his book *Savage Inequalities* to improve my understanding of his philosophy about how the American education system is not always fair or equal, particularly for kids in urban schools. I'm also reading a book by Barry Lopez called *About This Life* because I like his nonfiction work about nature and the environment. He's given me lots to think about in terms of the overall science curriculum.

This question is an attempt to discover two things: how well-rounded you are, and whether you stay up to date with current trends. This is an oft-asked question, so you should always be ready for it. Principals want to know if you plan to continue your self-education after you leave college and if you are willing to expand your horizons beyond the classroom. If you're not reading one or two books in the weeks prior to an interview, start right away.

#18:   Compared with other student teachers, how would you rate yourself?

A: On a one-to-five scale (as used on the state evaluation form), I consistently achieved an average of 4.7 on all five areas of student teaching competence. My cooperating teacher consistently rated me high on all the necessary markers for student teaching. While I know that student teaching is still a learning process, I achieved evaluative marks and comments that were some of the best. I like to set high standards for myself, just as I do for my students. Always learning and always getting better are goals I always want to be working toward.

Be honest and sincere when you answer this question. If you have some numerical data or written reviews to share with the interviewer, please do so. It's data that can easily be verified later. If your scores or evaluative marks are not as high as you would like, let the interviewer know that one of your primary goals is to keep improving. In short, you're not a "finished product"—you are still a "work in progress."

#19:   How do you define success?

A: My definition of success is student-centered. I want each student to succeed to the best of his or her abilities. My challenge is to identify student strengths and weaknesses and provide an individualized curriculum that will ensure maximum growth and development—not just in academics but in life as well.

This is a great opportunity to state (or restate) your goals and objectives. Don't make this a long response; a succinct and specific answer will garner more points than one that lays out an extended educational manifesto.

#20:   What aspect of your teaching style would you like to change?

A: Like many teachers, I guess I have a tendency to ask far too many low-level questions. I've learned that students become more involved in a topic when they are asked more high-level questions. Analysis, synthesis, and evaluation questions provide additional thinking and problem-solving opportunities for students. I'm working hard to make sure I include more of those kinds of questions in each and every discussion I have with students.

Never try to come across as the "perfect teacher." You are just beginning in this profession, and the interviewer knows it. He or she knows that you have some "rough edges," and he or she wants to know if you are aware of that. Take the time before the interview to list some of your minor issues or concerns and (specifically) what you are doing to alter or change them. Show that you are always improving; that you are always trying to be a little bit better than you are.

#21:   Do you believe you're qualified for this position?

A: Absolutely! I had terrific experiences in all my college methods courses. I was exposed to several different philosophies of teaching from some very exciting and engaging professors. I actively participated in the student education association and effectively coordinated the annual teaching conference on campus. I especially appreciated all the learning opportunities I had as a student teacher. My college supervisor continually challenged me to be a better teacher, and my cooperating teacher was an absolute inspiration. I sometimes can't believe the incredible growth I've made as a teacher, and I want to continue that process here at Parkwood Middle School.

You may not be asked this question directly, but it's one that needs to be answered nevertheless. Be sure to exude confidence and poise in your response—the interviewer wants to know if you are sincere or are just trying to pull the wool over his or her eyes. Be sure to cite some specific examples of your qualifications that can be recorded on the interviewer's sheet of notes from the interview.

INSIDER TIP

Two of the biggest mistakes candidates make in an interview are to talk too much or talk too little. That's why it's important to practice your responses…a lot!

#22:   What motivates you as a teacher?

A: I've had several inspirational teachers in my own schooling…all the way from Mr. Simpson in elementary school to Mrs. Madison in high school and Dr. Frobish at Big State University. I want to be that force in the lives of students—presenting myself as a model of learning, as someone who teaches by example and inspires through purposeful instruction.

Examples and specific details work well here. Don't talk in generalities, but rather offer two or three concrete examples of your own motivation. Don't cite theories from textbooks; instead, share personal beliefs and personal examples.

#23:   What is the greatest asset you will bring to the teaching profession?

A: From a very early age, I've always considered myself a passionate learner. Whether it was learning how to ride a bicycle, learning a foreign language, or learning about a new piece of technology, I've always been excited about learning. I enjoy the challenge of learning new material and ideas, and perspectives on old concepts. I believe I can bring that excitement and passion into my classroom. I believe I can model the joy, the thrill, and the enthusiasm I have for learning with my students…not just every so often, but every single day. If my students see my excitement for learning, they will also be excited about it.

This question is one of self-awareness. Be sure you are able to diagnose your personal thoughts and identify the attributes that will make you an outstanding teacher. Focus on one or two strengths and how those strengths relate directly to teaching. Your ability on your skateboard may be one of your skills, but it isn't related to teaching…and should not be part of your response.

#24:   What do you like best about teaching? What do you like least?

A: For me, teaching is an incredibly rewarding career! It offers unlimited possibilities to influence generations of students, imparting to them the excitement of learning, the passion of discovery, and the magic of an inquisitive mind. I believe that teaching is both a science and an art. It is also a way of making a difference in the lives of others. It is the shaping of minds and the shaping of futures.

What I like least would probably be the fact that I have a limited amount of time to work with my students. I have only 180 school days and seven-and-a-half hours in each of those days to share with them all the wonderful things they can learn. While I can't change the time I have available, I can change students' lives. I can't think of anything more exciting.

Don't select controversial topics for your response. You won't know where the interviewer stands on those topics, and you don't want to upset him or her early in the interview. Select topics that are non-controversial or non-confrontational.

#25:   What skills or abilities do you still need to develop?

A: I'd like to continue working on my DI skills. I know the power of differentiated instruction and was able to put it into practice during my student teaching experience. But I also know that it's not one of those skills a teacher learns overnight. While I had a great experience with Mrs. Walker, I'd like to talk with other teachers to see what else I can do to refine and solidify my DI skills for use in my own classroom.

If asked this question, don't select something that is obscure or theoretical ("I'd like to be better at teaching the *schwa* sound."). Select a skill that many teachers wrestle with and indicate that you consider this to be a long-term process—one that will demand both time and effort. Be clear that you are willing to invest that time and effort over the long term.

#26:   What three adjectives would you use to describe yourself?

A: The three I would select would be "passionate," "inquisitive," and "flexible." "Passionate" because I believe good teachers have a love for children *and* a passion for the subjects they teach…and I certainly have a passion for history. "Inquisitive" because I believe effective teachers continuously ask questions, looking for new explanations and answers. In so doing they serve as positive role models for their students, helping them ask their own questions for exploration. And "flexible" because I'm always willing to modify, bend, and adjust—never letting the little things, or the inevitable interruptions, get me down. This, I believe, gives me and my students incredible opportunities to succeed.

Show that you have the basic attributes of an outstanding teacher. While you may consider yourself to be an outstanding foosball player or the next great "American Idol" candidate, I'm sure you will agree that the interviewer would have a difficult time seeing the relevance of these descriptors to life in the classroom.

INSIDER TIP

One of the classic mistakes many candidates make is that they don't listen to the question. They are so anxious that they often begin answering the question before it's been fully asked. Slow down...listen...think! Then answer.

#27:   What three things really make you angry?

A: I get angry when a lesson doesn't go as well as it should. I put a lot of time and effort into each lesson, and I hold high expectations, not only for my students but myself as well. I also get angry with myself when my enthusiasm for a science lesson isn't there. I know that classroom teachers need to be good role models for their students, and one of the best ways to demonstrate that is through my own enthusiasm for learning. But, sometimes, with science, it just isn't there, and I know that's not fair for the kids. Science was never one of my favorite subjects in school, and I have to work at making it always exciting for my students. And, finally, I get angry when we run out of time. Sometimes my students and I are really getting into a lesson—they are working hard on some hands-on, minds-on activities in social studies, for example, and we see that it's almost time to get ready for the buses. I sometimes wish I had another hour or two in the school day in order to get everything in.

This is a terrific question, and your response will say a lot about who you are as a person. Don't ever make the mistake of blaming anyone else for your anger. Don't blame kids, colleagues, administrators, former professors, your cat, your parents, or your friends. The key is to take full and complete responsibility for your actions and for your anger. Make sure the things that anger you are school-related and that they are within your control to change.

#28: **Tell me something about yourself that I didn't know from reading your resume.**

A: You may not know that I've been tutoring a young man from Chile who is attempting to learn English so he can get his driver's license. I met Juan Carlos through my work at the YMCA and have been working with him for the past seven months. He's still struggling with basic English, but I've been able to find some good materials through the local literacy center. Fortunately, I can speak a little bit of Spanish, so we are able to communicate. It's been a tough road, but he's making some great progress now and hopes to take his driver's exam very soon.

This is not the time to repeat the obvious. Think about a skill, a talent, or an experience that doesn't quite fit on the resume, but which signals you as someone willing to go the extra mile or do an extra job. What makes you unique or different from all the other candidates applying for this same position?

#29: **How would your college supervisor (or cooperating teacher) describe you?**

A: He would probably use two words to describe me—"dynamic" and "persistent." I'm a person who is always on the go, someone who is willing to try new things, new approaches, and new strategies. I guess I'm never satisfied with the status quo. For example, our third-grade students were having difficulty making connections between their background knowledge and the information in a story during their reading lessons. I asked my cooperating teacher if I could use a strategy called "Concept Cards" to help students see how the knowledge we bring to reading is as important as the knowledge we get from reading. It took me about a week to set up this new approach, and it worked beyond our wildest dreams. It was a struggle at first, but I stuck with it and now all the third-grade teachers are using it. It was a great experience for the students and a great opportunity for me to apply some book knowledge in a practical way.

Pick something positive that your supervisor or cooperating teacher would say about you, but be honest. You can bet that your interviewer will ask this person the same question. Then, to support your point, describe a very specific example of how you solved a problem or tackled a difficult situation. Provide specific details about how your efforts contributed to improved student performance. Describe the strategy or approach and the specific results you obtained.

#30:   How will you complement this school?

A: I particularly enjoy an environment in which there is a great deal of camaraderie and support. My two previous visits to Deer Valley High School revealed that teachers here are quite supportive of each other. There are book-discussion groups, teacher-led in-service meetings, and several social events throughout the year. There is a spirit of cooperation and collegial support throughout the school, a spirit I can embrace and prosper in.

One of the essential "ingredients" in every new employee is the ability to work well with others and the ability to be part of a highly functioning team. The interviewer wants to know how you will become part of the "education team" and that your personality will complement the staff already in place. This is an opportunity to assure the interviewer that you are a true "team player." You'll also note that this is a good question to determine whether you have done your homework on the school prior to your interview.

———————

#31:   What are some of your hobbies or leisure-time activities?

A: I guess I've always been an "outdoors nut." I really enjoy getting outside and hiking, camping, and exploring nature. Last summer I hiked down into the Grand Canyon and spent three days traversing Rocky Mountain National Park in Colorado. Next summer I plan to spend a week hiking the Appalachian Trail from Maine down into Pennsylvania. I've read Richard Louv's book *Last Child in the Woods* and strongly believe that nature should be an important part of every child's education. I'd like to share my passion for the outdoors with my students.

This is another opportunity for you to sell yourself, not just as a teacher but also as a well-rounded individual. Be sure to emphasize any hobbies, activities, or pursuits that might carry over to the classroom. And be sure to let your passion for these activities show through.

FROM THE PRINCIPAL'S DESK:
"Smiling, friendly, joyful, excited, energetic, and enthusiastic are emotions and conveyances I look for in a candidate."

———————

#32:   What motivates you to be a teacher?

A: I've been very fortunate to have several inspirational teachers in my scholastic career, teachers who have challenged and motivated me to be a dynamic educator. These were teachers like Mr. Hoffman in eighth grade, who set a consistent positive example, and Miss Semple in tenth grade, who showed me that learning can be a lifelong pursuit. I've been motivated in ways I never thought possible, and I'd like to inspire and help others do the same.

This question provides an interviewer with some inside information about your reasons for becoming a teacher. They want some assurance that you're not just looking for long summer vacations and an easy 9-to-5 job. This would be a perfect opportunity to provide some specific details about people who have influenced you and your commitment to "keep the fires burning" throughout your teaching career. Don't be vague or uncertain here; offer compelling details and sound motivation.

#33:   How do you deal with stress?

A: I went into teaching knowing full well that it would be a stressful profession. During my teacher education program, I have developed several strategies to deal with the day-to-day stressors that inevitably come with the job. I visit a health club four times a week. On weekends I take long "power walks" through the woods near where I live. I'm learning about yoga and some of the benefits it offers to help individuals achieve a sense of harmony. I belong to a book-discussion group, take watercolor classes at the local art association, and have an active circle of friends. I try to maintain a wide diversity of physical and mental options that help me achieve balance in my life.

Don't make the mistake of saying that you are not stressed by teaching—the interviewer will know, right away, that you are less than honest. He or she has had numerous years of experience as a former classroom teacher and will know that stress is an inevitable part of the job. Let the interviewer know that you understand that stress and teaching go hand in hand, but also share the strategies and techniques that help you maintain a balance in your life.

#34: **What special skills or talents will you bring to your classroom?**

A: I've always been interested in theatre. I was in a number of plays in college and served as a youth director for a production at a repertory company in town. I've read some books about reader's theatre and how valuable it can be as a language arts activity, how it can help kids become more fluent readers. I would like to make it part of my language arts curriculum. From what I've read, I think it can be a positive addition to the classroom curriculum and a way to get kids more actively engaged in their own learning.

Once again, the interviewer is providing you with an opportunity to demonstrate how well-rounded you are. Don't blow this chance to let your personality and talents show through. As before, select examples that can have a connection to what goes on in a classroom or to specific elements of the overall curriculum. Let your talents and skills shine, but don't go overboard.

#35: **We have a number of applicants interviewing for this position. Why should we take a closer look at you?**

A: More than just a major in college, teaching for me is a passion. I've worked closely with our local Boy Scout troop, volunteered as a youth leader in my church, and spent quite a bit of time in the children's department in the local public library. With me, you'll get passion and commitment, but you'll also get a wide range of experiences in several different settings…experiences that give me a broad base beyond course work and student teaching.

This is a question often asked near the end of an interview. It is a great way to put a punctuation mark on who you are and what you will bring to a school. It's similar to the question, "Why should we hire you?" and provides you with a terrific opportunity to leave the interviewer with a most favorable impression. Practice this one, and be prepared to offer specific details. Your response should also answer the question posed in Chapter 6. One other thing: Don't "talk negative" about the other candidates; if you do, you're toast!

#36: **What are the three courses you took that shaped the teacher you will be?**

A: I took "Teaching Elementary Science" from Professor Sunday. She got me excited about inquiry-based science education, an approach that stimulates student questions and offers opportunities for students to pursue answers to their own self-initiated questions. In "Teaching Elementary Social Studies,"

Dr. Hansen taught me about the value of "hands-on, minds-on" teaching—not only providing children with necessary information, but giving them an opportunity to do something with that information. I also took "Topics in Children's Literature" from Dr. Smithton, who showed me the value of a literature-rich curriculum. I discovered some incredible books that I can use in all subject areas, not just reading. These three courses, and these three individuals, showed me that teaching can be dynamic and practical for each and every student in a classroom. They are lessons I will never forget.

Celebrate not only the courses that made an impact on your philosophy, but the people who taught those courses, too. If they are as good as you say they are, it is very likely the interviewer will know who they are (by reputation, at least) and will know how they have influenced other teachers hired by the district.

INSIDER TIP

Interviewers are most interested in hiring your *strengths* and *achievements*. They especially want what you have done or what you can do—not simply what you believe, or feel, or think.

#37:   **What sets you apart from the crowd?**

A: I guess you could say that I'm success-oriented. I really like it when my students succeed—not just one or two, but when everyone has the chance to improve in some selected area, whether that is social studies, science, music, or language arts. I've been known to create several different versions of the same lesson plan—my own differentiated curriculum—so that every child has the opportunity to enjoy some measure of success. My friends would say that success is my passion; my college supervisor says it's part of who I am. It's something I hope will be part of every lesson I create and will make a difference for every child I work with.

Don't sound arrogant with your answer to this question, but display a sense of confidence. This would be a good opportunity to bring in the perceptions and evaluations of others, particularly those who have observed you during your student teaching experience. Your answer should also be short and pithy; never drone on about everything you did during student teaching or in your pre-service field experiences.

#38:   **How would your best friend describe you?**

A: I've known Brian ever since we were in seventh grade together at Carbondale Academy for Boys. He would probably say that I was determined, because I'm always setting goals for myself and working to make sure they are all accomplished. He would also say that I have a unique sense of humor, particularly puns, because I'm always trying to manipulate words and phrases in humorous ways. And he would also say that I'm a hard worker. Once I start a job, I just can't let go until it's finished.

A good response to this frequently asked question is to focus on three personality features that carry over into the classroom. Traits such as hard worker, goal-oriented person, accomplished musician, and good listener are all indicative of good teachers, and you should bring these kinds of traits to the attention of the interviewer. Don't share traits (even though they may be true) that are not classroom-related. Your ability to dismantle the engine in a '57 Chevy or ride a Brahma bull for a minimum of eight seconds are not classroom-related attributes. Decide ahead of time on the three talents or personality dynamics you want to emphasize—particularly as they relate to classroom life.

———————

#39:   **What do you want to achieve as a teacher?**

A: I want my students to achieve to the best of their abilities. I want them to be successful, not just in mathematics, but in life. I want them to see how math touches every aspect of our lives, how it helps us solve problems, tackle difficult assignments, and think more clearly. I want to be more than just a math teacher—I want to motivate, model, and inspire; I want to make a difference in both mathematics and everyday life.

State your philosophy clearly and succinctly. This is a question that taps into your true reasons for teaching, whether you've given thought to your future, your educational and career goals, and your aspirations. Don't hedge on this one; plan it out ahead of time. It will definitely come up in one form or another.

———————

#40:   **Why do you want to teach?**

A: I had a professor in college who always used to say, "To learn is to change." That saying really captures a feeling that has always influenced me simply because I see all the positive changes that have occurred in my life through education. I want those changes to be part of what I share with young people. I want students to see how education can keep us current, keep us growing and changing throughout our lives. It's not the accumulation of knowledge that is important; it is what we do with that knowledge that keeps change happening, and that keeps us growing. I want to initiate and fan those flames in my students as much as my teachers have done in me.

Provide some evidence that you have given this question serious consideration. Make sure a sincere and committed desire to teach comes through loud and clear. Every principal has heard "Because I want to make a difference in kids' lives." Try something new, something that refers to a specific reason or incident in your life that propelled you into education. This would be a good opportunity to weave a short anecdote or personal story into your response.

✔**EXTRA CREDIT**

The "small talk" at the beginning of an interview is critical. It helps establish a conversational tone for the rest of the interview. Respond to questions with something more than a "yes" or "no." Be sure to ask your own questions that will require something more than a "yes" or "no" from the interviewer.

#41:   What personal skill or work habit have you struggled to improve?

A: Early in my student teaching experience, I often found it difficult to say "no." I volunteered for everything. I guess I just saw so many jobs that needed to be done that I jumped in and wanted to do them all. I soon saw that this was taking time away from lesson planning, classroom management, and individualized instruction. Now, instead of trying to be all things to all people, I try to tackle those ancillary duties that will have the greatest impact on student learning. I haven't perfected that yet, but I'm much better now at managing my time.

This is a good opportunity to highlight a task or chore that popped up early in student teaching. It would be appropriate to select something that everyone struggles with—time management, lesson planning, classroom management—and ways you tried to improve yourself as a result. Don't select something that is personal ("I have anger-management issues with three of my ex-boyfriends."); instead, select something that is universal to all teachers.

#42:   What three expectations do you hold for yourself?

A: When I'm teaching children, I always want to be fair and consistent. I know that fairness isn't about treating everyone the same; it's giving each student what he or she needs. I also want to be flexible. I know that no two teaching days are the same, and I need to be able to bend, adjust, and modify at the proverbial drop of a hat. If I can't change when something comes up unexpectedly, then I may be cheating my students out of some wonderful learning opportunities. But, above all, I expect myself to be a good role model for children. I want to display all the joy and excitement I have about education and let my students be part of that enthusiasm. I've always believed that good teachers are good models, and I never want to forget that in any classroom or academic activity.

This is the flip side of 'Why do you want to teach?" Can you provide the interviewer with three concrete reasons why you entered this profession? Can you convincingly explain, in a few short sentences, your motivation for teaching?

#43:   What are your professional goals for the next five years?

A: First, I want to attend graduate school and get my master's in curriculum and instruction. Beyond that, I would like to continue to take graduate courses and in-service courses so that I can stay current in the field. Second, I would like to attend a number of regional and national conferences so that I can connect with other middle school teachers in addition to staying up to date on the latest strategies and techniques for teaching at the middle school level. Third, I would like to contribute to some professional magazines and journals. One of my college professors helped me prepare a paper for submission to a student publication, and I guess the writing bug really bit me as a result. I'd like to write some articles and share my ideas and thoughts on teaching social studies.

Have a plan of action; if you don't, the position will probably be offered to someone else. Make sure that your plan includes a focus on the school's needs. Don't say that you want a graduate degree because you'll make more money; rather, say that you want to attend grad school in order to stay current and make more of a contribution to the school.

INSIDER TIP

Don't begin any graduate work until after your second year of teaching. You need time after your undergraduate work for your brain to decompress and rejuvenate. Your first two years of teaching will take all your time and attention, and you don't need to be distracted with the academic requirements of one or more graduate courses. After your second year of teaching, you will be much better prepared to tackle graduate work and to see its direct implications in your classroom.

C. Education, Training, and Experience

#44:   **Why did you choose education as your career?**

A: I chose education for three reasons: First, I wanted to be a positive role model in the lives of youngsters; second, I wanted to impart wisdom and an excitement for learning; and, third, I want to influence this next generation of students, imparting to them the excitement of learning, the passion of discovery, and the magic of an inquisitive mind. For me, teaching is a way of life rather than just a way to make a living.

Be short, succinct, and passionate. Two to three sentences filled with excitement and desire will provide the interviewer with a very positive message about who you are and why you are sitting in the interview chair.

#45:   **What new skills or ideas do you bring to the job that other candidates aren't likely to offer?**

A: I'm keenly aware of how the new standards are impacting classroom teachers. I know how teachers struggle with the implementation of those standards simply because I was asked to do the same in my student teaching experience. I learned very quickly that standards-based education is much more than possessing a knowledge of the standards; it's a commitment to an ideal, a philosophy that can have a significant impact on student learning.

This question provides you with a unique opportunity to demonstrate your knowledge of current issues, concerns, or initiatives in education. It is not really a question of how much better you are than others, but rather one that shows how knowledgeable you are about the wider world of education. If the competition is good, then this question (and your response) should let the interviewer know that you're bringing something extra to the position. Don't fall into the trap of comparing yourself to others ("I'm more qualified than anyone else because…."); instead, show what you do know (and let the interviewer make the comparison in his or her head).

#46:   How do you stay current in education?

A: Beyond my courses and my work with the student education association, I subscribe to *Instructor Magazine*, try to read at least one new teacher-resource book every month, and participate in an educational blog geared for new teachers. I know that my education doesn't end in the college classroom, but rather should be a continuous part of my growth and development as an educator.

Careful! If you are not prepared, this question—as simple as it sounds—could trip you up. The intent is to see how much value you have placed on your own education. If you give any indication that your college career is the end of your education, then you may be dooming your chances for employment.

#47:   Why did you attend _____ College?

A: I went to Mountain State College because of its strong teacher education program. In high school, I looked at several different colleges, and I considered the strength of their pre-service programs, the teaching expertise of the faculty, the student orientation, and the intensity of the coursework. Conversations with teachers in the area showed that Mountain State had a strong program, one that was both respected and admired. After a round of college visits, I was convinced that Mountain State would be the institution that would help me best achieve my goals. As I look back, I knew it was the right choice then and is certainly the right choice now. I got a great education, learned more than I ever knew possible about teaching, and was challenged at every turn. I don't regret a single moment.

Your answer should confirm your commitment to teaching. It should highlight your career goals, your passion for teaching, and how the institution helped you become a more accomplished educator. The interviewer will undoubtedly know about the status and reputation of the institution; it will be your job to show how the institution played a significant role in the pursuit of your goals. Your answer must also demonstrate that you make rational and conscious choices that demonstrate your ability to make (and follow through on) long-range goals.

#48:   What were some of the things you didn't like about student teaching?

A: I was sometimes frustrated about the time schedule. The periods were all divided into 90-minute time frames. My students and I would sometimes really get into a topic, and then we'd have to end because the bell rang. I found it upsetting that there wasn't always sufficient time to cover all the material *and* provide students with enough guided practice to put that information into practice. It sometimes seemed as though we were prisoners to the clock. But it did teach me about time management and the fact that I need to provide complete lessons in a designated time frame. That's something I continue to work on.

The best way to answer this question is to respond with something that has absolutely nothing to do with your abilities or your performance. Identify something that is outside your control—the clock, the bus schedule, the constant entrance and exit of students throughout the day, or the lack of adequate classroom computers. Make sure your response is about something over which you had no control.

#49:   What were the most rewarding aspects of student teaching?

A: One of my professors always used to say, "The best teachers are those who have as much to learn as they do to teach." I discovered that to be a good teacher one always has to be open to new strategies, techniques, and possibilities. Student teaching made clear to me that just because I have a lot of "book learning" doesn't mean that I know everything about teaching. Not only did I have to keep up on the latest information about biology education, I also had to be open to suggestions and comments from other teachers, administrators, and even students. Keeping an open mind was critical to my success as a student teacher, as I'm sure it will be to my success as a high school biology teacher. I don't believe there's such a thing as a finite body of knowledge; good teachers are always searching for new information and are always willing to consider new possibilities.

Administrators want to hire people who are not only consummate teachers but are well-rounded as well. This question provides you with a unique opportunity to demonstrate your personal philosophy as well as your professional philosophy. Your response should show evidence of both your teaching competence as well as your long-term potential.

> ## FROM THE PRINCIPAL'S DESK:
> "I particularly dislike candidates who ramble on and on about themselves or communicate that they are 'in love with themselves.'"

#50:   What experiences have you had working with students other than student teaching?

A: For the past three years, I have been a volleyball coach at the local YMCA, working with the junior volleyball team. I have been an after-school tutor at the Valley Community Center on Thursday evenings, helping youngsters with various homework assignments. Each summer I am a volunteer reader at Long Valley Community Library, where I share books and stories with three to five year olds. I've been a camp counselor for four years at the Big Mountain Nature Camp, and I've helped supervise playground activities during the annual Spring Fling in Centerville. I guess I've always been attracted to being around kids and take every opportunity I can to work with kids, teach them, and be a positive influence in their lives.

The interviewer wants to know if you've had varied and diverse opportunities in working with children. Have you experienced diverse populations of kids and been involved in an eclectic array of child-centered activities? Bottom line: The more programs and activities you've experienced—beyond student teaching—the better your chances at obtaining a teaching position.

#51:   Describe a teacher you admire.

A: I've always admired my fifth-grade teacher, Mrs. Voitman. In spite of a physical handicap, she always brought her best to the classroom. She never made excuses, never slacked off even if it was easy, and always gave every lesson and every student her best. She was a model of determination, effort, and positivity and probably, more than anyone else, made me see that good teaching is much more than memorizing standards or teaching long division.

Identify an educator who has made a positive and significant impact on your life and your chosen career. Cite two or three qualities or attributes of that individual that make him or her stand out. Make it clear to the interviewer that these specific qualities are those you embrace and those you believe are essential to good teaching.

D. Classroom Environment

#52: **Describe how you will deal with different cultures in your classroom.**

A: Good teachers are always sensitive to their students' cultural backgrounds. They respect students' languages, customs, traditions, and beliefs. They never make fun of students who are different, but rather celebrate these new opportunities for enriching the learning experiences of all children. One of the most effective ways of doing that, I've discovered, is through the use of relevant children's literature. Reading books about people from different cultures, developing units about customs and traditions in various parts of the world, and exposing students to the beliefs and ways of immigrants from various parts of the world can be some of the most effective ways of helping students understand and appreciate the multicultural world we live in. I had the unique opportunity to develop and teach a thematic unit on multicultural literature while in student teaching...and I'll never forget it!

In my discussions with principals around the country, this was a question that was quite often asked, in one form or another, in almost every teacher interview. Administrators expressed to me the fact that, in today's pluralistic society, teachers need to be aware of the many faces they will see in their classrooms and the ways in which those children can be informed and celebrated. Demonstrate (with specific details) how you have been part of this process.

#53: **Describe how you will make your classroom and the students comfortable.**

A: Students need to know that a classroom is their place; that it's not just the teacher's place into which they have been temporarily invited. If students have the impression that a classroom is "owned" by the teacher, they will be less likely to make an investment in learning. Classrooms that invite student engagement and celebrate the work of students are classrooms in which the best instruction takes place. Our classroom will be no different than a child's bedroom—a place where they will feel comfortable and can personalize, a place that values each and every occupant. To do that in our classroom, we will provide plenty of spaces to post student work. We'll invite students to suggest desk arrangements, color schemes, and decorations. As appropriate, we'll invite everyone to bring in personal items from home to use in the classroom. And we will celebrate students' different cultures and countries of origin by decorating with artifacts from those countries or cultures. Above all, we will promote a sense of ownership in the classroom as well as a sense of community.

Learning does not take place in a vacuum. You might be an excellent teacher and have exciting lesson plans filled with valuable resources. You might even have motivated students. Still, the environment or classroom in which all that is to take place will determine, to a large extent, how successful you will be as a teacher. Be prepared to discuss your plans for *your* classroom environment.

———————————

#54:   Describe an ideal classroom.

A: I believe an ideal classroom is composed of five basic elements. These include 1) Learning occurs best when the development of positive attitudes and perceptions is made part of every learning task. 2) Knowledge is best learned by making connections between what is known and what is to be learned. I always want my students to understand what it is to construct meaning. 3) I believe that, for learning to be effective and meaningful, students should be provided with opportunities to use and apply knowledge in practical situations—that is, to have opportunities to apply that knowledge. 4) We know that in an ideal classroom students learn best when they need knowledge to accomplish a goal they consider important. This often involves problem-solving, decision-making, and inquiry-based learning. And 5) in that ideal classroom, teachers can help students develop the mental habits that will enable them to learn on their own. Critical-thinking activities and metacognitive practices help ensure this. While these five principles are all part of that ideal classroom, they are also goals or aspirations I see for myself and my students. That ideal classroom may not always be achievable, but it can certainly be a realistic goal.

Demonstrate your knowledge of educational principles and practices that can be part of every teacher's classroom. Detail those items, and show how they can serve as goals for your future classroom. The interviewer wants to know your thoughts on two things: 1) What good teaching is; and 2) What kind of teaching you will practice.

———————————

#55: **To establish a positive classroom environment, share what you will do the first few days of school.**

A: Those initial days of a new school year are critical, as well as anxious—especially for ninth-grade students. Some of the things I would do would include 1) meeting and greeting my students at the door to my classroom. I want to shake their hands, call them by name, and welcome them into the room. 2) I want to establish a seating pattern or seating chart early on. I'd want to assign them to desks alphabetically, at least initially, so I can learn their names quicker. 3) I would want to talk briefly about myself, sharing with students my own education, my family, and especially my philosophy of education in general and English education specifically. 4) I'd want to take attendance each day, making sure I add a positive comment about each student as I begin learning their names and the correct pronunciation of those names. 5) I would also share an initial set of rules and classroom expectations—no more than five in number—and invite them to help establish additional classroom procedures throughout the year. Finally, 6) I would inform students about my expectations for each class and each period. They need to know my expectations about bringing textbooks, note taking, homework assignments, and appropriate behavior. I know it's a tall order, but one that will be essential to the eventual success I envision for each and every student.

Here's an opportunity to answer two questions in one. First, what is your philosophy of teaching? And, two, have you sufficiently thought about and planned out those critical first days of school? You want the interviewer to know that you have planned ahead, not that you've just made up the answer right there on the spot.

> ✔**EXTRA CREDIT**
>
> Interviewers always appreciate problem-solvers. Tell the interviewer how you can help him or her solve professional problems, and you'll always be ahead of the pack.

#56:   **Talk about the physical attributes of a classroom.**

A: I know that effective teaching depends on environmental factors just as much as on psychological, social, and personal factors. The way I lay out my classroom and the ways my students perceive that classroom will have a major impact on their level of comfort, their willingness to participate in learning activities, and, most important, their behavior. I want the classroom design to send a very powerful message to students. I want them to think, "This is a comfortable place that supports my needs, both physical and psychological, and one in which I feel secure and respected. I enjoy being here." I realize that where students learn is just as important as what student learn. In short, what I put into my classroom is as significant as what I put into every lesson.

The interviewer will want to know if you have given sufficient thought to all aspects of teaching, all the aspects that might influence the academic success of your students as well as your own teaching success.

#57:   **If I walked into your classroom, what would it look like?**

A: The desks in the classroom would be arranged in a horseshoe pattern. This will open up the front of the classroom for oral presentations, skits, and small-group work on the floor. My desk would be pushed into a corner in the back of the classroom, instead of being in the front. I know that a desk can be perceived as a symbol of power; its placement in the front of the room is a symbol of power and authority. I much prefer an atmosphere of shared governance in my classroom. I would soften up all the straight lines and sharp angles with lots of rugs, bean bag chairs, perhaps an old sofa, a variety of plants and animal habitats, and some pillows in a reading center. I have learned that all those lines and angles can sometimes be psychologically inhibiting for students and that rounded edges, lines, and corners suggest psychological safety and comfort for youngsters. My classroom would also have well-designed traffic patterns, allowing students opportunities to easily get to the pencil sharpener, the wastebasket, and from their desks to me, the door, and an activity center. Those patterns need to be based on both safety concerns as well as ease of accessibility. Most important, I want the classroom to be a community, one in which students are given opportunities to suggest patterns, arrangements, and configurations. Those opportunities will help build a sense of personal ownership in what we do and learn.

You probably haven't given much thought to the physical arrangement of your classroom. It, too, will provide the interviewer with some insights into your personal philosophy as well as your ability to plan ahead, so be prepared to discuss your ideas.

#58:   Talk about time management.

A: For me, good time management is all about transitions—you know, those times during the day when I move from one activity to the next. But in order for those transitions to be effective they need to be taught. For example, I would let students know when an activity will end ("We'll have the whole class review of triangles in two minutes."). I'd let students know what they can expect in any subsequent or follow-up activity ("After lunch, we're going to continue looking at the structure of onion cells."). And I'd be sure my lessons had clear beginnings and endings. I'd review the lesson objectives before the lesson begins and again at the conclusion of the lesson. Actively involving students in time-management procedures helps ensure a fully functioning school day and curriculum.

Show that you understand the importance of time management. Provide the interviewer with specific examples of how you will put time-management principles to work in your own classroom.

E. Student-Centered Questions

#59:   What do you enjoy most about working with young people?

A: I particularly enjoy their natural sense of curiosity—the way they ask questions, pose problems, and look at the world. One of the most powerful books I read recently was *Last Child in the Woods* by Richard Louv. In that book, he talks about how nature can help foster a lifelong inquisitiveness in children. Simply by taking kids on walks, exposing them to the natural flora and fauna of their neighborhoods, and stimulating them to question the world they live in, we can help students maintain their curiosity about things around them. I want to foster and stimulate that innate sense of curiosity through an inquiry-based curriculum that supports and enhances the questions children constantly seek answers for.

Here's another question where your passion for teaching will come through, either loud and clear or soft and indistinct. Let the interviewer know you are in it for the kids—and not for anything else.

#60:   What would you do with a student who has ADHD?

A: ADHD students comprise about 3 to 5 percent of the school-age population. These are usually students who have difficulties with attention, hyperactivity, impulse control, emotional stability, or a combination of several of those factors. Some of the techniques and procedures I would use in working with these students would include 1) Making my instructions brief and clear and teaching one step at a time; 2) Carefully monitoring work, especially when students move from one activity to another; 3) Adjusting work time so it matches attention spans; 4) Providing a quiet work area where students can move for better concentration; 5) Combining both visual and auditory information when giving directions; and 6) Whenever possible, breaking an assignment into manageable segments.

Students with ADHD offer significant and often perplexing challenges for many beginning teachers. Any administrator will want to know—given the number of ADHD students in his or her school—how you plan to teach this population of children. After all, there may be as many as 35 million children in the United States under the age of 18 with ADHD. Therefore, ADHD students will be in your classroom, and you need to know how to teach them.

#61:   What can you tell me about inclusion?

A: The idea that special-needs children, whenever and wherever possible, should be included in all activities and functions of the regular classroom, is known as inclusion. It is common, therefore, to find many classrooms with students of all ability levels working and learning together. For me, inclusion also means that students of all abilities, talents, and skills are offered learning opportunities that can occur between and among different individuals. I believe that inclusion is the total involvement of *all* students in an educational setting that best meets their needs, regardless of background or level of ability. It also means that I need to include my special-needs students in regular classroom activities to the fullest extent possible.

You will be asked a question about inclusion! No ifs, ands, or buts! Review your notes, read a course textbook, talk with teachers—but make sure you know this topic inside and out. In today's diverse classrooms, you will be expected to provide for the needs of every student; a principal wants assurance that you are aware of this expectation and that you can deliver the goods.

#62: **How would you differentiate your instruction to meet the needs of your diverse learners?**

A: During my student teaching experience I had the opportunity to work with several special-needs students. I quickly learned that there are some generalized strategies that I always need to keep in mind. These would include 1) Being aware that special-needs students may not want to be singled out for any special treatment. To do so may identify their disability for other students. 2) I need to consider learning over a long period of time. I realize that special-needs students may require extended periods of time to master a concept or learn a specific skill. 3) I need to be especially careful not to fall into the trap of focusing on the weaknesses of special-needs students. It's vitally important that I seek to identify the individual strengths of each student. And 4) I want to provide opportunities for students of all abilities to learn from each other. I want to be sure that everyone feels like he or she is contributing. I know that all that is a tough order, but I'm eager for the challenge.

Be sure you demonstrate your knowledge of special-needs students, their instructional needs, and your willingness to teach them. Always convey an aura of "positiveness" and enthusiasm in responding to this question. Demonstrate that you are eager for both the challenge and the opportunity.

INSIDER TIP

It's always appropriate to talk about a setback or disappointment you've had in working with students. But it's even more important to show how the experience made you a much better teacher today.

#63:   **What are you going to do for that kid who just "doesn't get it"?**

A: Never give up! I believe that every child has the right to an education, and each and every child should be provided with educational opportunities that are geared to his or her needs, interests, and abilities. If there's one thing that the concept of differentiated instruction taught me, it's that through assessments and learning profiles I can provide tiered activities that will offer each child a measure of success. My challenge is to discover to what tier the child should be assigned and the best practice strategies that will offer him or her the greatest opportunities to succeed. But, most important, I will never give up on any child.

Here's a great opportunity to show your passion and desire to teach. Keep your response positive, and be sure to inject some current research or best practices into your answer.

#64:   **What are some strategies you plan on using to teach learning-disabled students?**

A: I am aware that learning-disabled students will present me with some unique and distinctive challenges. Therefore, it is important for me to remember that LD students are not incapacitated or unable to learn; rather, they need differentiated instruction tailored to their distinctive learning abilities. Some of the strategies I plan to use include 1) providing learning-disabled students with frequent progress checks so that I can know how well they are progressing toward an individual or class goal and 2) giving immediate feedback to my learning-disabled students so they can see quickly the relationship between what was taught and what was learned. 3) Whenever possible, I need to make my activities concise and short. Long, drawn-out projects are particularly frustrating for a learning-disabled child. And 4) I know that learning-disabled children need and should get lots of multisensory experiences. A multisensory approach will help these students learn to the best of their abilities. I'm confident I can address the specific needs of the learning-disabled students in my classroom.

Here's another question that frequently arises in teacher interviews, for both elementary and secondary positions. This is another opportunity for you to show both a breadth and depth of knowledge about special-needs students. If you are "running neck and neck" with another candidate, your detailed and specific response to this question will always tip the scales in your favor.

#65:   What are some teaching methods used in full inclusion classrooms?

A: I like the One Teach One Support method. Students sit in rows in front of the chalkboard. As the teacher, I would station myself off to the right or left of the students in order to provide extra help and support as needed. In this model, the participants are all following my instruction so that no child is excluded. I could also use Station Teaching. Using this method, my classroom would be divided into two, even three, different sections. One group of students would be situated facing horizontally toward the blackboard; the second would be arranged vertically facing the right wall. If a third group is present they would be arranged parallel to their vertically arranged classmates and will be turned to face the opposite wall or the front of the classroom. Students with special needs will be divided among these groups evenly. A third method I could use would be Parallel Teaching. In this case my classroom would be arranged so that students are split into two groups. These two groups would be placed back to back, with students from each group facing me. One group would face me in the front of the classroom, and the other group would face the special education teacher in the rear of the classroom. Students with special needs would be divided equally between these two groups and their classmates, making sure that one group doesn't contain all the special-needs students. Of course, these aren't the only options I could use, but they are some of the most effective in terms of a full inclusion classroom.

If the answer above sounds detailed and specific, that is intentional. If I was a betting person, I could almost guarantee you that you'll get a question (or two) regarding inclusion, especially if you are an elementary teacher. Take the time and make the effort to know everything you can about inclusion. Otherwise, it's lights out…for you!

#66:   What are some of the challenges of inclusion?

A: Based on my experiences in student teaching as well as those I've had during my field experience requirements, I believe there are four primary challenges teachers need to be aware of. These would include 1) The danger of a two-system situation; that is, a clear and distinct separation between general and special education. 2) Another challenge for me is to make sure that there is complete accountability and a process in place to collect data objectively. 3) One of the biggest challenges would be to ensure that my expectations for special education students are not artificially low or, even worse, non-existent. And, finally, 4) I need to ensure, and convey, a philosophy that my general education classroom would be not be disrupted if and when special education students are included. I know these are not easy challenges to deal with, but every one of my students must achieve a measure of academic success.

See my explanatory note for Question #65. Read it, and heed it.

#67:   How do you plan to individualize instruction?

A: The best way to understand individualized instruction is to look at how it is used in special education. An Individualized Education Program (IEP) provides the foundation for learning. Most IEPs are developed as a collaborative effort of students (when appropriate), teachers, parents, school administrators, and related-services personnel. Many schools are using IEPs with students who score below grade level on standardized tests. Some of the instructional strategies I plan on using to individualize instruction would include cooperative learning, journaling, peer tutoring, inquiry-based teaching, problem-based learning, "hands-on, minds-on" projects, simulations, and role playing.

It makes no difference if you are an elementary or a secondary teacher. Make sure you can address the concept of individualized instruction, particularly in terms of how you would implement it in your classroom.

> **FROM THE PRINCIPAL'S DESK:**
> "I'm most impressed with those candidates who maintain a student-centered focus during the entire interview."

F. Curriculum, Instruction, and Assessment

#68:   Tell me about a time when you didn't perform well in student teaching.

A: During my first weeks in student teaching, I commandeered each classroom discussion; I didn't allow students opportunities to pose their own questions. I was so concerned with getting through the entire lesson plan that I forgot to allow opportunities for some inquiry-based learning. When my college supervisor pointed that out, we were able to work out a plan that allowed for more student questioning. I quickly discovered that when students ask their own questions they are more involved in the lesson and, consequently, want to learn more about the subject matter. It was an important lesson for me, and I've never forgotten it.

This question is designed to solicit two answers: your ability to self-evaluate, and your ability to learn from your mistakes. The best way to respond is to use an experience from early in your student teaching experience or pre-service education, an incident based on inexperience. Provide a specific example of how you dealt with the incident and how that experience has become part of your philosophy of teaching.

#69:   Why should teachers use lesson plans?

A: Lesson plans exist for several reasons. 1) They ensure that students are taught what they need to know (as established by the school, the district, or the state). 2) They are an outline that allows teachers to prepare for and attend to individual differences between and among students. 3) They ensure that teaching is both effective and efficient so classroom time is used appropriately. 4) They provide others, such as substitute teachers, with an appropriate instructional plan. And 5) they serve as a way for teachers to evaluate their teaching effectiveness.

Lesson plans are one of the cornerstones of teaching. Be sure you can convince an interviewer that you not only know what they are, but also that you are keenly aware of how they should be used. Don't make the mistake of thinking that this is a "throwaway" question. It is anything but!

#70:   Please describe the steps you use to plan a lesson.

A: A good lesson plan provides an outline for the accomplishment of specific tasks, while at the same time allowing for a measure of flexibility in terms of student interests and needs. My lesson plans consist of several critical elements. First, there must be a set of specific objectives. I know that a well-crafted objective has two components: the students for whom the objective is intended, and the anticipated performance. Next, there must be an anticipatory set or motivational opening—that is, how I stimulate student interest in a topic or subject. Next, I must provide a series of guided practice activities. These should incorporate several elements, including specific instructional methodologies, creative-thinking opportunities, "hands-on, minds-on" activities, and various ways in which students can practice the desired behavior. There must be some form of closure to the lesson—a teacher summary, a student summary, or some type of lesson product like a poster, brochure, mobile, or portfolio. Finally, I need to address evaluation and assessment—not as something done solely at the end of a lesson, but rather as a concept woven throughout the entire lesson. Above all, I have to make sure that everything in a lesson is geared towards the identified objectives or a set of specific standards.

If you don't know how to write a lesson plan, you're going to have a very difficult time convincing any interviewer you are a competent teacher. Make sure you know all the elements of a good lesson plan...cold!

#71:   What's the most creative or innovative lesson you have taught?

A: During the fifth week of student teaching, I contacted a family friend at Prospect Hill Cemetery. He provided my fifth-grade class with a tour of the cemetery. When we got back to the classroom, we divided the class into several teams. One team worked on a PowerPoint presentation, another created a timeline of important events in the life of the cemetery from the Revolutionary War to the present, a third looked into burial customs from around the world, a fourth developed an annotated bibliography of books about death and dying, and the final team gathered oral histories from some of the docents and volunteers at the cemetery. What was originally conceived as a three-week project eventually turned into a two-month multi-disciplinary project that combined social studies, art, music, language arts, and reading into a most exciting thematic unit.

This is a grand opportunity to provide a specific and concrete example of how you went "above and beyond" the usual lesson planning for student teaching. Be sure to provide specific details and any reactions you obtained from supervisors or administrators. Show, as much as possible, how you are willing to pursue projects that are somewhat out of the ordinary, projects that engage students in creative or innovative ways.

#72:   Describe a teaching strategy you use to maximize the learning potential of all students.

A: I particularly enjoy using K-W-L, the three-step framework that helps students access appropriate information in expository writing. It takes advantage of students' background knowledge and helps demonstrate relationships between that knowledge and the information in a text. When I use K-W-L with students, I want to involve them in three major cognitive steps: accessing their background knowledge about a topic (K), determining what students would like to learn about that subject (W), and evaluating what was learned about the topic (L).

Demonstrate your knowledge of common and familiar teaching strategies by describing a specific technique and its overall value for students.

✔EXTRA CREDIT

The following statements are always appropriate:

- "I'm sorry. I'm not sure I understood the question. Would you please ask it again?"

- "I'm sorry. I thought of a better answer to that question. I'd rather answer it this way...."

#73:   What is RTI, and what are its advantages?

A: Response to Intervention (RTI) is a multi-tiered service-delivery model designed to bring together educational specialists to provide high-quality instruction and interventions matched to student needs. RTI monitors progress frequently to determine effectiveness of research-based interventions and uses this data to guide instructional decisions. There are several advantages to RTI, including 1) It identifies the teacher as the first line of early intervention, 2) It uses data to inform and guide instruction, 3) It divides interventions into tiers of instruction, 4) It monitors a student's progress over time, 5) It increases the likelihood of student success, and 6) It provides behavioral interventions as well as academic ones.

RTI is one of the current "hot topics" of public education. Your knowledge of this topic should be thorough, complete, and comprehensible. You won't be able to make up an answer to this question; you need to know your facts. Do the necessary homework.

#74:   What can you tell me about differentiated instruction?

A: Differentiated instruction is a concept that makes it possible to maximize learning for all students. It is a collection of instructionally intelligent strategies based on student-centered best practices that make it possible for teachers to create different pathways that respond to the needs of diverse learners. The basic premise of differentiated instruction is that students are different. Indeed, students differ in 1) how they learn best; 2) what interests them; and 3) readiness for the content. Teachers of effective heterogeneous classrooms recognize the similarities and differences in students and proactively plan for these differences.

Another "hot topic"? You bet! Do your homework…please!

FROM THE PRINCIPAL'S DESK:

"One of the best candidates I ever interviewed was able to give excellent examples of how she would differentiate for specific needs at the T-1 and T-2 levels."

#75:   What is standards-based education?

A: A standard is a description of what students should know and be able to do. By definition, educational standards let everyone—students, teachers, parents, and administrators—know what students are expected to learn. Standards are designed to answer four basic questions: 1) What do we want students to know and be able to do? 2) How well do we want them to know and do those things? 3) How will we know if students know and can do those things? and 4) How can we redesign schooling to ensure that we get the results we want? Standards are designed to help students be responsible for their own learning, become good thinkers and problem-solvers, and know what quality work looks like. Standards-based education engages students, not only in the learning process but also in knowing what is expected of them.

Your response to this question should be direct, detailed, and descriptive. Don't try to "wing it." Make sure you know exactly what you're talking about and that you clearly understand all the necessary terms.

#76:   Please describe the difference between content standards, benchmarks, and performance standards.

A: Content standards describe what students should know or be able to do in ten content areas: language arts, mathematics, science, social studies, fine arts, health, physical education, world languages, career and life skills, and educational technology. Benchmarks make clear what students should know and be able to do at four different grade spans: K to 3, 4 to 5, 6 to 8, and 9 to 12. Performance standards answer the questions "What does good performance look like?" and "How good is good enough?"

As with the previous question, know your "stuff." Show that you've done your homework ahead of time and that you are knowledgeable about the role of standards in curriculum design and effective teaching.

#77:   What can you tell me about reading-comprehension instruction?

A: Many teachers subscribe to the notion that reading involves an active and energetic relationship between the reader and the text. The reader-text relationship is reciprocal and involves the characteristics of the reader as well as the nature of the materials. This is often referred to as a transactional approach to reading, and it is based on two primary principles successfully used by teachers around the country. First, reading is a lived-through experience or event. Children "evoke" the text, bringing a network of past experiences with the world, language, and other texts. Second, the meaning is neither in the child nor in the text, but in the reciprocal transaction between the two. This approach highlights three critical stages in the reading process: 1) Before Reading—This involves those processes designed to link students' background knowledge to text; 2) During Reading—These are processes designed to help students read constructively and interact with the text; and 3) After Reading, the processes designed to deepen and extend students' responses to text.

If you are an elementary teacher, you *will* be asked questions about the teaching of reading. Count on it! If you are a secondary teacher, you should also prepare yourself with information about reading instruction in the content areas. It could make a difference.

#78:   What is a balanced reading program?

A: A balanced reading program is one in which students are provided with direct instruction, a support structure, and opportunities to utilize reading strategies in meaningful text. In short, they are encouraged, supported, and sustained in many literacy activities throughout the entire elementary curriculum. These activities can be divided into eight categories: 1) reading aloud to children; 2) shared book experience; 3) guided reading; 4) individualized reading; 5) paired reading; 6) sustained silent reading;

7) language exploration; and 8) reading and writing. A balanced reading program occurs when teachers work to integrate reading into all subject areas and all parts of the instructional day. It's an opportunity for students to see reading as an integral foundation of the overall curriculum.

Again, know (or re-learn) how reading is taught. Be prepared to express both the breadth and depth of your knowledge. Make sure you know what you're talking about.

#79:   What can you tell me about guided reading?

A: Guided reading is the heart and soul of the reading program. It is a time to teach students the strategies used by accomplished readers and to involve students in the dynamics of quality literature. It is an opportunity for students to create a positive relationship with texts by combining what they know with what they can know. Fountas and Pinnell have defined guided reading as "a context in which a teacher supports each reader's development of effective strategies for processing novel texts at increasingly challenging levels of difficulty." I believe the implication of this definition is that teachers guide students (via appropriate reading strategies) through increasingly more difficult reading materials in order to achieve higher levels of comprehension and greater independence in reading. One of the major differences between guided reading and more traditional forms of reading instruction is that guided reading is conducted within small, flexible, and ever-changing groups.

Know how reading is taught. No excuses!

#80:   How would you handle varied reading abilities in your classroom?

A: RTI combines universal screening and high-quality instruction for all students with interventions targeted at struggling students. First, it is important to screen all students for potential reading problems at the beginning of the year and again in the middle of the year. Teachers need to monitor the progress of students who are at risk for developing reading disabilities. Next, differentiated instruction should be provided for all students based on assessments of their current reading levels (Tier 1). Next, teachers should provide intensive, systematic instruction on up to three foundational reading skills in small groups to students who score below the benchmark on universal screening. Typically, these groups will meet between three and five times a week for 20 to 40 minutes (Tier 2). Third, the progress of Tier 2 students should be monitored at least once a month. This data can be used to determine whether students still need intervention. Finally, intensive instruction should be provided daily in order to promote the development of various components of reading proficiency to students who show minimal progress after Tier 2 small-group instruction (Tier 3).

Repeat after me: "Do your homework on reading instruction!"

✔EXTRA CREDIT

Avoid using tentative terms such as "I think," "I feel," or "I guess." Over-use of these terms tends to leave a less-than-positive impression with the interviewer—that you are unsure or indecisive. Interestingly, psychological research has demonstrated that women tend to use these terms more than men.

#81: How will you integrate technology into your classroom?

A: The number-one use of technology comes in the form of research. The Internet, for example, provides students with a wealth of current information on any topic or any subject. I want my students to experience the incredible array of data available in any subject area. A second project that can help integrate technology, while truly getting the students excited about school, is Web site creation. I plan to publish a Web site with my class about information students have researched or personally created. This might include literary efforts, results of scientific investigations, critiques of books read, or problem-solving projects. I also want to explore the possibility of online assessment for my students. If students have the opportunity to demonstrate what they have learned through the use of technology, then I have more time available to teach. It's an exciting new concept I'm eager to explore. Still, I have to remember what one of my professors said: "The program should not be built around technology; rather, technology should be built into the program."

Most of the administrators I talked with want to know how versed teacher candidates are in technological issues. Your response to this question should demonstrate your awareness of and comfortableness with technology as a powerful teaching tool.

#82: **How will your students' overall performance improve as a result of technology?**

A: I believe my students' performance will improve in three specific areas. One, students will have increased opportunities to become more actively engaged in the dynamics of a lesson. Technology will offer them an array of information available nowhere else. Second, I believe technology will help me help my students improve their thinking skills as well as their problem-solving abilities. Through the use of technology, we will be able to focus on higher-level thinking skills that go beyond rote memorization into discovery and exploration. And, third, it will provide me with some incredible opportunities to differentiate my instruction. I'll be able to use technological resources to target specific students with specific instructional options. I was able to incorporate all these concepts into a unique project during my student teaching experience. The project, which we named "Explorers for Hire," was developed as part of our social studies unit on the exploration of the New World. Students had to obtain information from the Internet about specific explorers and write personal biographies. They each took on the role of a specific explorer and applied for a selected exploration in the form of special documents and records, mapped and tracked their routes of exploration, planned their voyages and the supplies they would need, and reported the results of their exploration. The students embraced the project enthusiastically, and it generated a new interest in social studies.

In your response to this question, you need to include two things. One, you must demonstrate your knowledge of technology and its instructional advantages. And, two, you must provide the interviewer with a specific example of how you put those principles into practice. In other words, you must be able to "talk the talk and walk the walk."

FROM THE PRINCIPAL'S DESK:

"We once interviewed a young lady who told us she was well-versed in technology; she told us she could operate a CD player and use an overhead projector."

#83: **What is your philosophy regarding homework?**

A: I believe that the value of homework is threefold. One, homework helps students develop good study habits. Two, especially if it is interesting and relevant, homework fosters positive attitudes toward school. And, three, homework communicates to students that learning happens in and outside of school.

You should anticipate getting one or two questions regarding homework. Different schools have different philosophies about homework, and it would certainly be to your advantage to know what the homework policy is of a school you are interviewing with long before the interview. You'll find it much easier to answer this question if you do.

#84:   How much homework will you assign your students?

A: In our "Curriculum and Instruction" course, we learned that there is a positive correlation between homework as a learning tool and student achievement in the classroom. However, we also learned that the amount of homework assigned needs to be tailored to the students' age and grade level. So how much homework should I assign my students? Although there is no definitive answer, I'd like to use a simple formula that Dr. Graber shared with us. That is "Homework = Grade Level $\times$ 10." This means that the amount of after-school homework (in minutes) is equal to the grade taught times 10. Since this position is for fifth grade, that would mean that I would assign approximately 50 minutes of homework per evening (5th grade $\times$ 10 = 50 minutes), including all subjects collectively: reading, math, science, and social studies.

It is always to your advantage to cite some pertinent research, a professor, or another authority in the field. This lets the interviewer know that you just didn't make up your answer on the spot, but that you are aware of some evidence to back up your response.

#85:   What would you consider to be a good homework assignment?

A: Many students think homework is a form of academic punishment. They will often ask, "What does this have to do with anything?" Thus, it would be important for me to ensure that there is some kind of connection between the homework I assign and the real world. In short, students need to understand the "why?" in each homework assignment—and the "why?" is not something like, "Because I told you so." In student teaching, I tried to help my fourth graders see the relevance of mathematics to their everyday lives. Examples of homework assignments I used included the following: 1) Find 15 items in your house that are rectangles; 2) Select one of your mother's favorite recipes and double it; 3) Use a menu from a local restaurant, and plan a meal for four people within a budget of $50.00; and 4) Locate a chart or graph in the local newspaper, and explain what it means in words. I discovered that this "real-world" connection was also a great motivational aid.

The interviewer wants to know if you've had personal experience in putting all your "book knowledge" into practice. Plan to answer this question with specific examples and anecdotes from your pre-service training.

#86:   What is the purpose of assessment?

A: Good assessment is multi-disciplinary and multi-faceted. It should be designed to address four major concerns of every teacher. One, it should provide meaningful feedback; that is to say, are students learning what I'm teaching? Two, it should be used to effectively measure instruction; in other words, is the instruction tailored to the individual needs of students? Three, assessment is used to evaluate progress—are students progressing in a satisfactory manner? And, four, assessment must inform instruction. That is to say, it must be used to help develop appropriate activities that will ensure student success throughout a course or topic. In adhering to these four basic concepts of assessment, I use tools such as projects, demonstrations, portfolios, rubrics, and writing samples to help me effectively gauge each student's progress and performance in a lesson.

Count on it! You will be asked a question about assessment and its value in a lesson or unit. Prepare yourself well for this query, because it will come up in one form or another. Review those notes you took a few semesters ago, or get a copy of that textbook on assessment and evaluation. Know that this is a critical question and one that every good teacher—both elementary and secondary—should be prepared to answer.

#87:   What is the difference between assessment and evaluation?

A: Assessment is when teachers gather information about students' level of performance or achievement. Evaluation is comparing a student's achievement with other students or with a set of standards. Although there are slight differences between these two terms, I also believe there are several similarities. Both assessment and evaluation should be continuous and ongoing processes. So, too, should a variety of tools be used in order to provide the most accurate gauge of students' learning and progress. Good evaluation and assessment are also a collaborative activity between students and teachers. However, most important, both evaluation and assessment need to be authentic—they must be based on the natural activities and processes students do in both the classroom and in their everyday lives. Overall, I like to think of evaluation and assessment as processes that offer opportunities for growth—teacher growth, students' growth, and program growth.

Here's another question that's sure to pop up. This is a unique opportunity for you to showcase your knowledge of this topic and how you plan to address it in your own classroom. If you've done the necessary research, you should have no problem. If you haven't, well....

INSIDER TIP

The best way to establish rapport with the interviewer is through frequent eye contact. Eye contact signals the interviewer that you are interested and that you are trustworthy.

#88:   How do you know students have learned what you taught them?

A: Evaluation is an integral part of the learning process. As such, it must be sensitive to the needs, attitudes, and abilities of individual students as well as the class as a whole. I must be careful that I do not over-rely on one form of evaluation just because it is easy or convenient for me to use. Rather, I need to use a multi-faceted evaluation program if I am to determine whether students are mastering the objectives for each lesson. To that end, I need to use formative evaluation measures in order to assess student progress with the material being presented, as diagnostic instruments to determine student strengths and weaknesses, and to provide student and teacher feedback. I also need to use summative evaluation measures at the conclusion of a unit of study in order to assess the extent of pupils' achievement, to provide a basis for the calculation of course grades, and to provide data from which parent reports and school transcripts can be prepared.

I like this question—and so do a large number of principals. Your response demonstrates the extent of your knowledge about assessment and evaluation, your plan for putting that knowledge into practice, your understanding of the connection between lesson objectives and student performance, and your comprehension of both product and process evaluation. It's a tall order, but one you need to master.

G. Discipline, Motivation, and Classroom Management

#89: **What principles do you use to motivate students?**

A: I recall one of my college professors discussing this topic in considerable detail. Specifically, motivation is comprised of three critical elements. First, I must always provide instruction that will ensure a measure of success for every student. That is, every student must know that he or she can achieve a degree of success with an assignment or academic task. Second, I need to create a community of learners in my classroom, one that celebrates all its members and provides a supportive, inspirational, and motivational environment. Third, students must see a value in what they are learning. During student teaching, I found that, for motivation to occur, students must know the reasons, rationale, and whys of any learning task. When I provided students with specific reasons on why they needed to learn about the Articles of Confederation, for example, they were more engaged and more motivated. I want all my students to see a connection between what they learn in the classroom and their lives outside that classroom. That's true motivation!

Many prospective teachers mistakenly believe this to be a "throw-away" question, one that anyone can answer. Not so! You need to tell the interviewer that, no matter what grade or subject you plan on teaching, you are aware of the basic principles of motivation and how you will make them part of your classroom curriculum.

#90: **How would you motivate an unmotivated student?**

A: I remember Rodney, one of the students in Mrs. Rooney's classroom. Rodney was a completely unmotivated student; he couldn't have cared less about learning, and he couldn't have cared less about school. He was there only because he had to be. As a student teacher, I was assigned to work with Rodney. My assignment was to motivate him, to get him interested in Life Science specifically and in learning in general. I went back to all those notes I took in college and developed a plan based on five key elements. First, I involved Rodney in a combination of both individual and group projects. Second, I periodically invited him to meet with me and discuss any barriers to his individual learning. Third, I provided him with numerous opportunities to set his own goals in Life Science. We made sure those goals were realistic, and we started with tiny steps before moving to larger ones. Fourth, I always modeled my enthusiasm for learning. I always portrayed myself as an eager and enthusiastic learner. And, fifth, I provided Rodney with frequent offers of help. The change wasn't immediate, but we began to see some improvement in Rodney's behavior and his academic performance after several weeks on this new program. Rodney discovered that he had an innate love for Life Science—especially when we focused on wetlands creatures. I think the whole experience was beneficial for both of us.

Motivation is a critical factor in how students learn. Yet make no mistake about it: You *will* have unmotivated students in your classroom! Make sure you convey your awareness of the importance of this issue as well as specific ways you plan to deal with it. Always relate your response to an individual or incident you experienced in your pre-service training.

#91: What is your philosophy of classroom discipline?

A: I would want to establish a specific set of rules for students to follow. This set of rules would be designed to create a sense of order and comfort so that teaching and learning can take place. But, in order for the rules to be effective, I know they need to be built on some very basic principles. These principles would include 1) Students should have a sense of ownership of the rules; they should be invited to contribute a set of expectations about classroom behavior. 2) Classroom rules should always be framed in positive terms. Instead of "Don't hit people," I would say "Respect other people." Instead of "No talking when someone else is talking," I would say, "Take turns talking." 3) I would make sure all students understand the classroom rules through concrete examples, specific anecdotes, and personal stories. And 4) I would make sure my classroom rules were consistent with school rules. Above all, my classroom-discipline policy would be structured on a set of rules that would be communicated in clearly defined terms and language students understand, provide the specific rationale or reason for a rule, and offer concrete examples of each rule as I would want it practiced.

Discipline is one of the most important concerns in schools today. You should definitely plan on being asked a "discipline question" at some time during the interview. Your response should be carefully crafted in terms of specificity and purpose. The more detailed you are in your response the better you will be viewed by the interviewers. Never talk in generalities when responding to this query. Be precise!

INSIDER TIP

Always think about the interviewer, and gear your responses toward his or her concerns. If you can demonstrate how your talents or experiences can address one or more of his or her concerns, you will always come across as an interesting candidate as well as a first-rate teacher. Be outwardly oriented, and you'll always have a successful interview.

#92:   How do you handle discipline problems?

A: One of the most important lessons I learned early in my pre-service training was the fact that, when students act out, teachers should always admonish behaviors rather than personalities. In other words, instead of saying, "I've had it with you, Carla. You're always late!" it would be far more appropriate and far more productive to address the behavior. For example, "Carla, your tardiness disrupts the class and makes it difficult for me to begin a lesson." By focusing on the behavior, the student is given the opportunity and responsibility to make a change. When teachers punish the student, rather than the behavior, then that responsibility is taken away. And I definitely want my students to be responsible.

Here's another question that frequently comes up. In responding, as in the previous question, be very precise and direct; don't try to make up an answer. It would also be appropriate to cite an example of when you had to discipline a student and what resulted from that encounter.

#93:   How would you involve students in the development of classroom rules?

A: I think it would be very important to take time at the beginning of the school year and invite students to contribute a set of expectations about behavior. During an initial brainstorming session, I would look for groupings or clusters of ideas. I would want to take time to talk with students about how they could combine their ideas and suggestions into very specific categories. These categories would include honoring personal space, respecting property, considering the feelings of others, paying attention, and using appropriate movements. The final list we would create would be a personal one for students simply because they helped create it. They will have that all-important sense of ownership and will be more inclined to follow the rules they helped create.

This question helps the interviewer determine if you will be an autocratic/dictatorial teacher or one who actively engages students in the affairs of the classroom. Be confident in your response and confident in your details.

#94:   What have you found to be the toughest aspect of discipline?

A: Consistency! I discovered in all my experiences with children that the key to an effective discipline policy in any classroom is consistency. For me, consistency means three things: 1) If I have a rule, I must enforce that rule. 2) I shouldn't hand out lots of warnings without following through on consequences. Lots of warnings tell students that I won't enforce a rule. And 3) I must be fair and impartial. I must be sure that the rules are there for everyone, and that includes girls as well as boys, tall people and short people, students with freckles and students without freckles, and special-needs students as well as gifted students. Maintaining consistency is, and will continue to be, a challenge. But it's a challenge I'm ready for.

The questions about discipline are many and varied. They can come in a number of ways. You need to be adequately prepared to respond to each of them in a way that demonstrates your knowledge of this all-important topic and the specific ways you plan to address it.

#95:   How would you handle a student who is a consistent behavioral problem?

A: One of the most powerful books I read was Thomas Gordon's *Teacher Effectiveness Training*. In the book, Gordon talks about the importance of "I" messages as a powerful way of humanizing the classroom and ensuring positive discipline. In student teaching I had the opportunity to practice delivering "I" messages. I recalled that every "I" message is composed of three parts: 1) including a description of the student's behavior ("When you talk while I talk…"); 2) relating the effect this behavior has on me, the teacher ("I have to stop my teaching…"); and 3) letting the student know the feeling it generates in me ("…which frustrates me."). I believe that the use of "I" messages has the potential for helping to change student behavior—not just for the short term, but for the long term as well. For example, when I began using "I" messages with Darren, one of our chronic talkers in class, I began to see some subtle, yet definite changes. By the end of my student teaching experience, Darren was able to control his excessive talking and make positive contributions to the class.

Careful! Don't make the classic mistake of answering this question with lots of negative words or examples. Rather, take the "high road"; relate some research and an experience that helped you to turn a student around. Don't describe the student in negative terms; rather show how you took a positive approach.

#96:   What steps would you take with a student who was disruptive in your classroom?

A: First, I would make sure my intervention was quiet, calm, and inconspicuous. For example, one day I saw that Michael was not paying attention in class. So I used his name in part of my presentation, as follows: "As an example, let's measure Michael's height in centimeters." Michael had been whispering to his neighbor. When he heard his name, he was drawn back into the lesson with no disruption of the class. I also believe that the more immediate a reprimand, the less likely a student will feel I condone his or her behavior. And, perhaps most important, reprimands should be kept brief. The more I talk, for example, the more I will distract from the lesson and the more I "reward" a student for inappropriate behavior.

This is another opportunity in which a personal example or anecdote will help to illustrate your point and your philosophy. Show the interviewer that you've had some first-hand experiences and that you knew how to deal with them. Don't even think about suggesting that the student be sent to the principal's office. If you do, you're dead!

FROM THE PRINCIPAL'S DESK:
"We have had candidates carry in suitcases of dusty art and materials they spread out all over the table. Some used it, but it was mostly overkill."

#97:   What, for you, is the most important aspect about discipline?

A: Discipline is not about getting students to do what I want them to do. That's what dictators do, and I don't see myself as a dictator. Discipline is providing an environment in which positive teaching and learning can occur simultaneously; it's order from within. To get that, I need to teach my students proper discipline. During the first weeks of school, I need to establish a set of expectations, the specific details of those expectations, and the consequences if those expectations are not followed. For me, nothing is more important than a well-crafted and well-articulated discipline policy. If it is true that "an ounce of prevention is worth a pound of cure," then the time I take at the start of the school year will pay enormous dividends throughout the rest of the school year.

Discipline questions always pop up in interviews, whether you are an elementary teacher or a secondary educator. Know discipline inside and out! Know discipline like the back of your hand, and know how to state your discipline policy clearly and compellingly.

#98: **What classroom-management techniques do you use or are you most comfortable with?**

A: I had a very interesting conversation with my cooperating teacher early in my student teaching experience. She gave me a piece of advice I've never forgotten and which I've used on numerous occasions. She said that teachers often make the mistake of using "stop" messages rather than "start" messages. For example, "Stop talking. We need to get started." A better message is "Get out your math books, and turn to page 44." I learned that a "start" message establishes a productive, businesslike tone for a lesson. The focus is not on the negative behavior, but rather on the importance of the lesson. When I began to practice that philosophy in my own classroom, I saw some tremendous changes—very positive changes, I might add.

This is a great opportunity to share a story or personal anecdote that demonstrates how you put a philosophy or concept into practice. It would be equally important to share how that opportunity helped you become a better teacher.

#99: **What are some things teachers do that create classroom-management problems?**

A: Teachers sometimes, inadvertently, create discipline problems through certain kinds of behaviors. Professor Lewiston shared some of the most common behaviors. These included 1) extreme negativity; 2) an excessively authoritative climate; 3) overreacting; 4) mass punishment; 5) blaming; 6) lack of instructional goals; and 7) not recognizing students' ability levels. I learned that avoiding these, and other similar behaviors, can go a long way toward creating a climate of trust and caring that will significantly reduce misbehavior.

Describe your knowledge of the inappropriate behaviors in addition to your own personal reaction to those behaviors. Let the interviewer know that you are aware of factors that may have a negative influence on students' learning and that you are conscious of what you need to do to avoid those behaviors.

#100: Describe the most challenging student you've experienced and how you dealt with him or her.

A: I'll never forget Dac Kien. He was one of those magical students who influence a teacher's life in a thousand different ways, a student we celebrate long after he or she leaves our classroom.

Dac Kien came into our classroom one damp January day. His family had emigrated from Vietnam, coming to this country to seek a better life. But they had a challenge; none of them could speak English. When Dac Kien arrived in our classroom, he had learned two words—"McDonald's" and "okay." As the student teacher, I was assigned the task of helping him learn English—the school did not have an ESL teacher.

And so we began to learn English. I read stories to Dac Kien, recording each one as I read. He then listened to those stories over and over again as both he and I pointed to each word as it was said. I created some word cards for him, using key words in the stories and printing the letters in large script. At first I selected concrete words like "cat," "house," "car," and "grass." Every day we practiced with those words, and every day we listened to more stories.

I selected some students from the class to become part of a "Distinguished Tutors" group. At various times during the day, each of these students would spend about ten minutes with Dac Kien, helping him learn the words and adding one new word each day.

Day by day Dac Kien's vocabulary increased, and week after week he was able to create simple sentences with his new-found vocabulary. All this was reinforced with some after-school time, during which Dac Kien and I would use some specific VAKT measures to reinforce and solidify his new vocabulary.

By the end of my student teaching experience, Dac Kien was able to speak in complete, although simple, sentences. There was a new confidence in his eyes and a new feeling of success in his life. I'll never forget when he told me, "Thank you; I learn much." It was only after that experience when I learned that "Dac Kien" in Vietnamese means "acquired view or knowledge." I know now that he wasn't the only one who acquired some new knowledge.

This may be the only time you want to "break" the rule about limiting your responses to two minutes or less. This is a great opportunity to demonstrate how you've made a significant impact in a student's life—not just academically, but affectively as well. Don't get overly emotional in relating your story; let the anecdote speak for itself. As with every other question in this book, be sure to do your homework, and plan to bring in a great story about one memorable student.

#101: How do you motivate reluctant readers?

A: Reluctant readers can benefit enormously from an integrated approach to learning. Some of the strategies I have used include 1) designing and developing activities in which reading and literature can become an inherent part of every curricular area—in short, making reading cross-curricular; 2) integrating the language arts throughout the entire curriculum, providing students with active opportunities to participate in both expressive and interpretive language arts in every subject area; and 3) engaging students in real-world activities: for example, reading different types of literature, writing letters and manuscripts for others to read, communicating with friends and family members, and listening to news broadcasts and public speakers. The value of this approach is that it underscores—particularly for reluctant readers—the competencies they will need long after they leave my classroom.

At the elementary level, the teaching of reading is critical. You can definitely count on several questions related to your views on how to teach reading, what to do about non-readers, and how you plan to deal with the diversity of readers in your classroom. Please go back and re-read the textbook(s) you used in your reading methods course(s). You'll be glad you did.

INSIDER TIP

Some interviewers try to maintain a poker face throughout the interview. Don't be intimidated, and don't assume that an expressionless face is a sign of displeasure. You may not be getting positive messages from the interviewer's body language, but that doesn't mean you should be anything but engaged, joyful, and enthusiastic.

H. Parents and Community

#102: What are some ways you would communicate with parents about students' progress?

A: I know from my earlier research that many teachers at West Wind Elementary School have their own classroom Web pages. I would want to develop my own Web page that would be updated weekly and would provide parents with regular information about stories to be read, books to be discussed, and specific ways they could encourage reading at home. I would also want to plan a regular sequence of phone calls to parents to let them know of the successes their children were having in school. I would want to celebrate those successes with parents on a regular and systematic basis. I would also like to visit many parents in their homes or in the community to informally or formally discuss strategies and techniques that would support the learning taking place in school.

If you will be teaching at the elementary or middle school level, you can certainly anticipate this question. While the topic may not have been covered in your pre-service training, it is one critical to your success as a classroom teacher. Be sure to have three specific ideas on how you would address parent participation and how you would make it part of your regular classroom routine.

———————

#103: Why is it important to communicate with parents?

A: I learned in one of my methods courses that as much as 70 percent of a child's intellectual development takes place at home. Therefore, it is critical for teachers and parents to work together, to establish a positive partnership that can support and enhance a child's academic growth—no matter what the age, the subject, or the grade. I was fortunate to be able to work with my cooperating teacher to establish an action plan for parent involvement based on school/home newsletters, a regularly updated Web page, a series of regular e-mails and phone calls, home visits, and structured meetings at school. When parents were provided with authentic opportunities to participate in the affairs of the classroom, students' achievement levels showed remarkable gains. It was a most valuable lesson.

As I said, if you are planning to teach at the elementary or middle school level, you will undoubtedly be asked one or more questions about parent involvement. This is a golden opportunity for you to describe your overall classroom plan for actively engaging parents in the scholastic lives of your students. Show that you have a plan, not just a philosophy. Be prepared to talk about some of the parental-outreach efforts you practiced during student teaching.

———————

#104: Describe how you would prepare for a parent-teacher conference.

A: First, I would send a personal letter home to each parent to confirm the day, time, and place of the conference. Then I would gather the records of each student—portfolios, work samples, writing samples, and homework papers. I would review my notes on each student's behavior, academic progress, and interactions with peers. I would clarify ahead of time who, exactly, would be attending each conference—is it the child's biological parents, a relative, a guardian, a grandparent, or a foster parent? If necessary, I would make arrangements for an interpreter for non-English-speaking parents. I would invite parents to bring in a list of questions, issues, or concerns. Lastly, I would make sure the conference was not conducted from behind my desk, but rather side-by-side at a table, so as to enhance conversation and a level of comfort.

Your response should demonstrate that you've given serious thought to this annual or semi-annual event (at almost *every* elementary, middle, or high school). Show that you are aware of the basic elements of a good parent-teacher conference and what you can do to inform parents and make them comfortable during the conference. On the surface, this may seem like a minor question, but it can further solidify your ability to plan ahead, rather than trying do things "on the fly."

#105: How will you involve the community in your classroom?

A: I would want to recruit lots of classroom volunteers. I would use the telephone, informal surveys, questionnaires, and face-to-face contacts to solicit parent volunteers. I would schedule a special orientation meeting to provide potential volunteers with a set of responsibilities and expectations. I'd give parents opportunities to observe the actual skills I would like them to perform, including marking papers, creating art materials, arranging community field trips, supervising small-group work, carrying out remedial tasks, creating bulletin boards, and duplicating classroom materials. I would also want to create a support system for parent volunteers. Parents need to feel they are working under a trained professional, and to do that I would schedule a series of round-table conferences so they could be up to date and feel part of a larger group. It would be challenging, I know, but it would all be worth it in the long run.

Among all the tasks you will face as a classroom teacher, one of the most challenging and also one of the most beneficial is how you will invite parents and the community to be part of the educational experiences happening in your classroom. (Secondary teachers, take note!) The interviewer wants to know if you are willing (and able) to go above and beyond the usual demands of teaching, and your answer to this question will provide a most appropriate response.

#106: What are some ways to let parents know about the positive things going on in your classroom?

A: I like "The Two-Minute Note." Each morning, I would write a short (two to four sentence) note about a positive event or accomplishment for a single student and invite the student to take the note home. I would start alphabetically with a student at the top of my grade book and then, each day, select the next student on my class list until I got to the bottom. Then I would start again at the top. That way, every student would take home one "two-minute note" each month. Not only would this method give me an opportunity to focus on the good things students do, but it also would notify parents about those positive events.

Give an example of how you keep parents informed about the activities taking place in your classroom. Provide a specific example, and convey your enthusiasm as you share the anecdote with the interviewer.

#107: How would you involve parents in the affairs of your classroom?

A: There are a number of things I would do, on a regular basis, to get parents actively involved in the overall curriculum. Here are just a few: 1) I would encourage parents to participate continuously throughout the entire school year. 2) I would use students as "recruiters" to get their own parents involved. 3) I would reward and/or recognize parents for their efforts, however small. 4) I would strive to be friendly, down to earth, and truly interested in parents *and* their children. And 5) I would continuously communicate to parents the fact that their involvement is ultimately for the benefit of their children.

Demonstrate that you have a plan—not just a vague idea. Show that you know what is involved and how it will become part of your overall program. Show your sincerity and eagerness to partner with your students' parents.

#108: What will you do if a parent challenges you?

A: Parents often challenge teachers when they don't have all the information or when they have the wrong information. Consequently, it would be important for me to put my "listening ears" on. I'd schedule a meeting with the parent either before or after school. I would provide the parent with an opportunity to vent his or her frustration and try to determine where that frustration came from. I would demonstrate some active listening. For example, if the parent said, "You're always giving my kid way too much homework!" I might respond with something like, "It seems like you're upset about the amount of homework Jillian is getting each night." I would never try to shout down a parent or do anything that would negatively impact his or her self-esteem. I want to work with the parent in reaching a mutually satisfactory solution.

You'll get angry parents. Be sure you know how to deal with them. Again, here's another opportunity to take "the high road" and show how you can turn a negative event into a positive one.

I. Career Goals

#109: Since this will be your first teaching job, how do you know you'll like the career path?

A: I've spent a lot of time in classrooms—field experiences, student teaching, and volunteer work at the elementary school in my hometown. I talked to several teachers here and throughout the district and asked them what they enjoy most about the Wide Open Spaces School District, and they all said they like the camaraderie and support system in place for teachers. I get a real sense that there is a spirit of cooperation and dedication here that is important in the education of children, but equally so in maintaining high morale and a vision for the future. I believe I can thrive in this type of atmosphere and am confident that my philosophy and that of the school will be a long-term match.

This can be a tricky question, but, if you have done your homework about the school or district, it can be answered with confidence and assurance. Let the interviewer know that you have seen teaching from many different angles. In addition, allow the interviewer an opportunity to see how your philosophy and that of the school are mutually compatible—that you are not just excited about teaching, but that you are especially excited about teaching in this particular school. Allow your enthusiasm and energy to come to the fore; demonstrate your passion through tone of voice, body language, and animation. Because this will undoubtedly be one of the final questions you'll be asked, make sure you put a large exclamation point on your response.

FROM THE PRINCIPAL'S DESK:
"The best-prepared candidates are those who did their homework on the school and can ask meaningful questions."

#110: What are your plans for professional growth?

A: Good teachers keep learning, continually adding to their knowledge base throughout their teaching career. My own education doesn't stop just because I've graduated and have a teaching certificate. If I am to provide the best possible education for my students, I need to provide myself with a variety of learning opportunities throughout my career. To that end, I plan to take several graduate courses with an eye towards getting my master's in math. I'm planning on attending several regional and state conferences so that I can begin developing a network of fellow teachers, both experienced and novice. I've recently ordered some new teacher-resource books recommended by one of my professors so that I can stay up to date on some of the new strategies for mathematics instruction. I must be a model of good learning myself.

Have you given some thought to what you plan to do after you get your degree? Please don't make the fatal mistake of assuming that you have all the education you will ever need to be an effective teacher. If you go into the interview with that attitude, I can promise you that you'll leave the interview with nothing more than a handshake and a pat on the back. Design your future! Write it down, and plan to insert it somewhere into the conversation.

#111: Who else are you interviewing with?

A: I've applied for primary-level teaching positions in six different school districts in Big Bear County. I currently have three interviews scheduled and hope to finalize a position within the next few weeks.

Don't shoot yourself in the foot by saying that you are interviewing for a position at the local YMCA, a position as a part-time counselor at an area youth organization, *and* a couple of school positions. You want the interviewer to know that you are absolutely and unequivocally committed to teaching. Don't make the mistake of sharing all the jobs and positions available in the area. Demonstrate that you are focused on and committed to a specific teaching position. Trying to impress an interviewer with a wide range of possible jobs—both in and out of education—will only backfire on you.

#112: Where do you want to be in five years?

A: After my first two years of teaching, I'd like to begin pursuing my master's degree in professional writing. I'd like to get involved in writing a teacher resource book or two, giving back to the profession in some way. And I'd like to be a continuing and positive influence in the lives of high school students, sharing with them the joys (and even some of the frustrations) of writing.

Too many candidates make the mistake of being wishy-washy with the response to this question. Provide the interviewer with two or three carefully chosen and carefully thought out responses. If you say something like, "Well, I just hope I'm still teaching here at Excellent High School," you have blown the answer. The interviewer wants to hear clear and concrete responses, an indication that you have given serious and sustained consideration to your future.

> **✔EXTRA CREDIT**
>
> If you don't understand a point, ask that it be restated or explained further. For example, "In other words, you would like to know...."

#113: What are your plans for graduate school?

A: I plan to devote my time and attention to being the best teacher I can for the first two years of my teaching career. I want to put all my talents and efforts into ensuring that I've mastered the curriculum, the day-to-day life of a successful classroom teacher, and the academic success of every one of my students. When I have that down, then I would like to attend Mount Merry University to obtain my master's in reading. I want to learn everything I can about the latest research and teaching strategies, particularly as they impact my students' comprehension development. I plan to spend about two years in obtaining my master's.

Have a plan. Interviewers want to know that, just like your students, you see yourself as a learner. Consider how a graduate degree will help you improve your teaching effectiveness and make additional contributions to the school.

J. Round-Up Questions

#114:   What concerns you most about teaching?

A: I have a real passion for, a real interest in, and a real concern about quality teaching. I want to maintain that passion throughout my professional life. I want students to be equally passionate about learning—as excited as I am. I want them to experience all the joys I've had as a student. To learn a new technique or strategy and then see it work in a classroom situation is absolutely thrilling for me. I want to help students experience that same level of enthusiasm in their academic pursuits.

Don't misread this question. Although you are asked about your "concerns," don't make the mistake of thinking that the interviewer wants you to discuss a negative. Use this question as an opportunity to discuss a "positive"—something that all good teachers think about. Make sure your positive attitude shines through loud and clear.

#115:   What is the most exciting initiative happening in education today?

A: For me, the most exciting initiative is the emphasis on differentiated instruction. DI is a way of teaching that relies on a toolbox robust enough to provide different learning pathways to a wide range of learners. I cannot say, for example, "I taught it, so they must have gotten it." What is critical for me is knowing the essential curriculum and the individual learners; plus developing the wisdom to know which developmentally appropriate strategy to use with whom. The challenge for me is to learn, and to be able to use, a repertoire of strategies that will make a difference in each student's learning.

Talk to your former professors. Read the latest journals. Consult with area teachers. Know what is happening in education today. And then show how you will address that initiative in your own classroom.

FROM THE PRINCIPAL'S DESK:
"If I ask 'Is there anything else you'd like to tell me?' I'm always impressed when a candidate—in two minutes or less—can effectively summarize the basic interview theme: matching his or her qualifications to my school's needs."

#116: If, for one day, you were empowered to make one change to the education system, what would it be?

A: Money! I would make sure there would be sufficient money to fund local schools and educational efforts. I'm not sure if that funding would come from property taxes, income taxes, or some form of government intervention, but I would create a system or policy that would ensure that schools got the money they needed—and that they were given the discretionary power to spend that money in the ways they think most advantageous for students.

Three of the "headaches" principals wrestle with every year are dealing with the budget, the quality of teaching, and test scores. Address one of those issues, and you'll have the interviewer's attention and, ultimately, his or her support.

#117: What characteristics make a master teacher?

A: I believe there are three qualities every outstanding teacher should have. First, he or she should be a constant learner. Teachers should realize that education is as much about the journey as it is the destination. Continuous learning is an essential ingredient in every teacher's career. Second, they need to develop a positive partnership with their students, to create a classroom that is truly a "community of learners" that supports and encourages learners of every stripe both cognitively and affectively. And, third, a master teacher must be willing to admit mistakes. Teaching is never a perfect science, and we will all make some mistakes along the way. Good teachers—just like good students—learn from their mistakes to become stronger, better, and more accomplished. I believe I have those three qualities.

The interviewer wants to know if you are aware of the qualities of outstanding teachers *and* how well you match those qualities. From your answer, the interviewer must be confident that you are keenly aware of the expectations of teachers and that your skills and talents are in line with those abilities and/or philosophy. If you are not directly asked this question, it would be a good one to use as a wrap-up to the interview, particularly in response to a question like, "Is there anything else you would like to say or add to this interview?"

INSIDER TIP

Never leave an interview without asking at least two to three questions of your own.

#118: If I hired you today, what would you do first?

A: First I would obtain the entire fourth-grade curriculum and all the associated textbooks. I would try to learn as much about the program as I possibly could. Next, I would want to interview several of the other fourth-grade teachers and see what challenges they have faced over the past year and how they have addressed some of those concerns. Third, I would pull out some of my college textbooks, or perhaps talk with one or two of my former professors, to review important information on classroom management and discipline. Above all, I would do my homework and make sure I was ready to "hit the ground running" on the first day of classes in August.

This is a good question that shows how well-prepared you are and whether you have thought sufficiently about the future. You can really solidify your standing with the interviewer by responding with a very concrete and well-planned response. Identify two or three specific points and why you consider them important. Show that you have thought about this question well in advance of the interview by being succinct, direct, and focused. The ability to plan ahead is a key factor in any teacher's success; show that you are one who can.

#119: What is your philosophy of education?

A: Lao-Tse once described an effective leader as one who imparts to his charges the feeling "We did it ourselves!" So it is in the realm of teaching and learning. I believe an effective educator does not simply disseminate facts and figures, but acts as a catalyst, teaching (by example) a love for learning. Via provocative questions rather than patent answers, children are led to discover knowledge; thus, they become active participants in the learning process rather than passive receptors. To be a successful "catalyst" requires a great deal. As a doctor selects the appropriate tool to execute a surgical procedure or an artist the correct brush to express a desired gesture, a teacher must have the knowledge and creativity to utilize a plethora of tools.

You will be asked this question—if not in the interview, then definitely as part of an application for the school or district. Don't prepare your response the day before the interview—prepare it now! Make it powerful, make it personal, and make it uniquely yours.

#120: Why should we hire you?

A: I assume you are looking for a teacher with a solid commitment to the field, one with an ability and a desire to work with students of all abilities and skills who can grow and develop over the years. I will bring to this position an incredibly successful student teaching experience, the desire and commitment of a well-rounded educator, and the desire to continue my learning well past my baccalaureate degree. My grades, recommendations, experiences, and goals underscore my passion for this profession and my desire to make a positive and long-lasting impact on the lives of my students.

You might think that this is the most stressful question you could be asked. Rather, you should expect that this is a question that will always be asked in one form or another. Make sure you are honest, specific, and sincere. Don't go on and on—show in four or five detail-rich sentences how you are the ideal match for the position. It is always appropriate to address one of the school's or district's concerns or issues in your response.

✔EXTRA CREDIT

The #1 Most Important Tip: Assess your strengths, and relate them directly to the needs of the school.

#121: What type of person would you hire for this position?

A: I would hire someone who had a broad range of experiences in working with young people, a commitment to further his or her education through readings, conferences, and graduate studies, and an awareness of the strategies, standards, and protocols essential to the teaching of American history. I believe I have those job requirements.

Don't be shy; at the same time, don't ramble. Provide two or three very specific philosophical points to the interviewer, and let him or her know that you are the one candidate who has those two or three qualities.

#122: Why should I consider you for the position?

A: Three reasons: One, I have an extensive array of experiences in working with children. Besides my student teaching experience, I have been a regular volunteer in the public library's after-school program, a counselor at the local Boys Club, and a summer intern at Bay City Children's Home. Two, I'm a team player. I enjoy working as a contributing member of a team, sharing creative ideas, and considering the ideas of others. I see a school much like a professional football team—we are all geared to a single goal, and that goal can only be reached when we all work together in harmony. Three, I'm excited about teaching and kids. I've wanted to be a teacher ever since fourth grade, and I want my own students to experience the joy of discovery and the thrill of self-investigation I have in my own education. Oh, and one more thing: I'm a fun person to work with!

Don't hedge your bets on this question. Provide the interviewer with three specific traits or abilities that stand out in your resume and that you can express with desire and conviction. Be sure to share ideas that go above and beyond the usual job qualifications. Before crafting your own personal response to this query, please go back and re-read Chapter 6.

#123: What do you think is the most difficult aspect of being a teacher?

A: Patience. One of the toughest lessons I learned is that change does not come about overnight. Just because I put together a dynamite lesson plan doesn't necessarily mean that every student will "get it" the first time around. Just because I make a sincere effort to involve parents in the affairs of my class doesn't mean that every parent will come on board. And just because I reprimand a student for some inappropriate behavior doesn't mean that he will change right away. I have to keep in mind that good teaching, like gardening, involves a large measure of patience. A gardener doesn't expect all his or her seeds to sprout at the same time; neither should a good teacher. I think that if I can keep that concept in mind then I'll be successful in this profession.

Here's an opportunity for a large dose of humility and an equally large dose of reality. Show that you've done some self-evaluation, and demonstrate that you've learned something in the process. You'll win a lot of fans that way.

#124: What things about yourself would you like to bring out that have not yet been discussed in the interview?

A: I have always lived by a simple motto: The best teachers have as much to learn as they do to teach! No matter where I am in my teaching career, I can always learn something more, master something more, and improve something more. I have long realized that my teacher education does not end when I graduate from college. In fact, that's when it begins.

As teachers, we have a multitude of responsibilities throughout our careers. One of the most important, I believe, is our own education. While we may be committed to the educational advancement of our students, we should be no less committed to our own lifelong improvement as a teacher. Education, for me, is an ongoing process rather than a final product.

Want to leave the interviewer with a good impression and be eager to have you sign a contract? Want to let an interviewer know that you are the one and only person he or she should hire? Then re-read the response above. By this point in the book you'll know why it's a good one.

FROM THE PRINCIPAL'S DESK:

"The best interview was when I was with a woman who could only talk about kids she had worked with in the past. She was able to describe the students, their parents, and academic abilities in great detail. Her love and joy came across so clearly as she 'teared up' when speaking of one of her students who was experiencing a crisis in his home and when she laughed with elation as she spoke of another student who went from a below-basic non-reader to a student who started discussing books he was reading over a pizza lunch with her."

CHAPTER 8

25 Zingers!
(and 25 Dynamite Answers)

It's inevitable—sometime during your teacher interview, you'll be thrown a zinger! It may be about a particularly difficult aspect of teaching; it may be about an education initiative or new piece of legislation; or it may be something about your background or experiences that you're not keen on discussing. These questions are full of stress, anxiety, and potential dangers. These questions seldom have single right answers; instead, the interviewer is interested in seeing how you think on your feet, how you handle yourself under stress, and how composed you are when presented with a situation that has no easy answers.

The most important thing to keep in mind is that you can always expect one of these "toughies." Knowing that you will probably get one or two is the best way to prepare for your interview. While you won't know the exact questions you'll be asked, you will be prepared for them in advance. In fact, one of the best ways to prepare is to invite a friend to ask you some of the questions below over a period of several days prior to a scheduled interview.

It's important to remember that these are intentionally stressful—you know it, and the interviewer knows it. Don't let your confidence be shaken—maintain your calm, poise, and positive attitude. This is not the time to become defensive or argumentative; it is the time to demonstrate that you can handle the inevitable stressors that teachers face on a regular basis.

Of course, when asked one of these zingers, you shouldn't tell the interviewer that the question is unfair or inappropriate. A defensive posture will work to your these questions to the best of your ability. Don't fake it; ed this question in many interviews, and he or she will ed to concoct a response that is insincere, inaccurate, ply don't know an answer to a question, pause for a few ver in the eye and simply and honesty inform him or ver that question."

Following are 25 "zingers" that frequently pop up in teacher interviews. Of course, these are not the only challenging questions you'll be asked, but if you practice with these you'll be ready for almost anything an interviewer can throw at you.

#125: Tell me (us) a little about yourself.

A: I'm a goal-oriented individual; I set high standards for myself and my students. During student teaching, I was given the opportunity to set up a behavior-modification program for my students. It was a tremendous success because students were given an opportunity to help establish some of the parameters. I also worked closely with parents to create a homework project that got them more involved in the math curriculum. Also, I'm on the cross-country team in college, and each year I set new goals that have helped me achieve personal bests in both the 5K and 10K.

This is often the first question asked in an interview and can also be the most dangerous. Don't talk about generalities, and don't offer information that can easily be obtained from your resume. This is an excellent opportunity to help control the conversation by providing the interviewer with information he or she may wish to explore later in the interview. The key is to stay focused and be direct. Never take more than two minutes to answer this open-ended question. If you do, they'll lose interest even before they ask the next question.

#126: Why do you want to be a teacher?

A: I'm passionate about kids. I've worked as a volunteer at the YMCA camp, I've coached a Little League baseball team, and I was a guest storyteller for one semester at Candy Cane Elementary School. I believe I can be a positive influence in the lives of children. One of my professors always used to say that teachers should be outstanding role models for children. I believe I'm a good model because I'm involved in the lives of kids—not just in the classroom, but in all those activities that take place outside the classroom.

This question is actually two questions in one. An interviewer is often looking for the response to "How dedicated are you?" and "How passionate are you?" If you can succinctly address those two queries, you will always impress an interviewer. Make sure the focus is on your specific reasons for entering the teaching profession. A response like "Many members of my family, including my grandmother, my aunt, two nieces, and my mother, have been teachers, so it seemed natural for me to become one, too" will always turn off an interviewer. Keep the focus on *your* reasons.

#127: What are your goals in education? Where do you see yourself five years from now? How does this position fit into your career plans?

A: First, I want to be the best teacher possible. To do that, I've set three primary goals for myself. I'd like a position that challenges me; one where I can continue to grow and develop as a teacher. Second, I'd like to be a positive influence in the lives of children at both the cognitive and affective levels. Third, I'd like to include the community in the total education of children. Based on what I have learned so far, I believe Running Brook Intermediate School offers me the best opportunity to accomplish those goals. I would hope to be here for many years—growing, learning, and contributing right alongside my students.

You can count on being asked this question in an interview. The interviewer wants some assurance that you plan to stay in the school/district for an extended period of time. This is also a great opportunity to answer the always unasked question (see Chapter 6), because your permanence in the school/district will relieve the principal of one more responsibility—having to hire another teacher. In short, the principal wants to know if you plan to stay in the position over the long haul and if you've given thought to the future beyond your first year of teaching.

#128:   **Describe a time in student teaching when you failed to resolve a classroom conflict.**

A: We had this student in second grade—Matthew—who was hyperactive. He was on meds, but his parents always forgot to give him his medication before he came to school. As a result, one of us had to maintain close proximity to Matthew throughout the day to keep him in check. In hindsight, I would have worked harder to establish open lines of communication with his parents. I would have created a more intensive classroom behavior-modification program that would have rewarded Matthew for good behavior. I would have focused more on those times when Matthew exhibited good behavior and would have established a concrete plan of action to record those successes.

A principal or interviewer wants to hear not just about the successes you've had, but also how you have dealt with some of the inevitable challenges of day-to-day teaching. Again, always focus on the positive; never blame a student or his parents. Show what you learned as a result of this experience and how you might use that experience to address a similar challenge in the future. Keep the spotlight on the fact that you are vitally interested in improving your teaching skills; that you are always willing to grow and learn.

✔EXTRA CREDIT

Make it a point to tell the interviewer some facts about yourself that show how you are different from all the other candidates. Instead of saying "I successfully completed student teaching," say something like "During student teaching, I helped establish a before–school 'Thinkathon,' helping kids with problem-solving skills." Always distinguish yourself from everyone else.

#129:   **What would you say are the broad responsibilities of a classroom teacher?**

A: A classroom teacher has to be many things, have multiple skills, and often be in two places at the same time. Teachers have to be good classroom managers and have a consistent and fair classroom-discipline policy. They must also be up to date on assessment and evaluation protocols and how to effectively integrate those into the overall curriculum. They must know how to motivate students, particularly reluctant learners, and develop relationships with administrators, parents, and other teachers. They need to be able to respond to the individual needs of every student in a classroom and be able to plan their time in an efficient manner. I believe I can bring that array of skills to the physics position here at Rainbow Trout High School.

You should plan on being asked this question in one form or another. It's designed to see if you have a realistic picture of the teaching profession or whether you have a "glamorized" view (e.g. "Well, I think teachers should be really nice people and should help all students."). The question should be answered with specific details and knowledge about the multiple tasks and duties teachers face every day. The interviewer wants to know that you have not unfairly "romanticized" teaching, but are keenly aware of the day-to-day responsibilities of teachers.

#130: How have you handled criticism of your lessons or teaching performance?

A: My college supervisor sometimes mentioned that I had time-management issues—that is, I found it difficult to get everything done that I had planned. Some parts of a lesson would go too long, and others didn't have enough time to develop. I learned that this is a common problem with pre-service teachers. So I took the opportunity to talk with some of the more experienced teachers in the school to see what kinds of tips or strategies they had that would help me master my time a little better. One of the best ideas I got was to list my lesson objectives on the board for students to see and then check them off as the lesson develops. That gave me—and the students—visual proof on how the lesson was progressing.

This question often provides the interviewer with insight into your accountability and professional character. How do you handle criticism—positively (as a learning opportunity) or negatively (the reviewer didn't know what he/she was talking about)? It would be most valuable to take this opportunity to demonstrate (with specific examples) how you were able to use that criticism to become a better teacher.

#131: Tell me about one of your lessons that flopped.

A: During my student teaching experience, I put together a science lesson on making homemade ice cream in a zip-loc bag. It was an activity I had learned in my "Teaching Elementary Science" course. The lesson was designed to demonstrate how liquids change into solids. I provided my students with the materials and a set of printed directions. Halfway through the lesson, I realized that I had listed the wrong amount of salt to use. The ice wasn't melting, and the milk mixture wasn't turning into ice cream. In fact, nothing happened. In hindsight, I should have practiced the activity at home. I explained to the students that scientists make mistakes all the time—in fact, there are many scientific discoveries (penicillin and the electric light bulb, for example) that are the result of unintentional mistakes. I wanted to let them know that even teachers make mistakes and that it's okay to flub up every once in a while. You could discover something new. Next time, however, I'll test any experiment before teaching it.

Every teacher has had lessons that bombed. Don't make the mistake of saying that you haven't had at least one or more "duds" in your student teaching experience. The interviewer will know, instantly, that you are trying to con him or her. By the same token, it's always a good idea to approach any disappointment or problem from a positive angle. Never blame anyone (but yourself), and always demonstrate how you were able to turn a potential negative into a positive. Demonstrate an ability to reflect on your mistakes and use those mistakes as stepping stones to become a more accomplished teacher.

#132: **What might your college supervisor want to change about your teaching style?**

A: I'm a detail person; my supervisor likes to look at the big picture. I would obsess over the smallest detail, the tiniest item, or the smallest bit of information, making sure that each and every piece was part of a perfect lesson. My supervisor tried to get me to look at the larger picture—the overall goals of a lesson or unit. While I'm still concerned about all the necessary details of a lesson plan, I've come to see the importance of where I'm headed in each lesson. I've learned that an eye on the standards—rather than simply the pebbles along the path—will often make the journey more productive for my students. My supervisor helped me appreciate the journey as much as the destination.

Here's a great opportunity for you to demonstrate how you handle criticism as well as how much you are willing to adjust your philosophy. Are you inflexible, or are you open to change and willing to look at a situation from a new angle? Whenever you are asked one of these questions, it's always a good idea to point out some minor difference of opinion rather than a major conflict. Equally important, demonstrate how you worked with someone on resolving the issue. Show how you can accommodate the ideas of others and especially how you can do that in a spirit of shared cooperation.

#133: Tell me about a situation that frustrated you during student teaching.

A: I was frustrated when my college supervisor made me write out my lesson plans for the first ten weeks of student teaching. Many of my friends only had to write complete lesson plans for the first four weeks and then they went to "block plans." However, in talking with my supervisor, I learned that it is always advisable to over-plan—that is, to write lesson plans that are more detailed and more involved early in the teaching process. I discovered the advantage of that on two occasions—once, when an assembly had to be cancelled, and another time, when a teacher on our social studies team called in sick at the last minute. I was glad to have those expanded lessons—they really came in handy. I understand now why I was asked to do a lot of over-planning early in my student teaching experience.

This question is designed to probe how you react to criticism. Are you someone who blames everyone else when things don't go right? Or are you someone who uses advice in a positive way to become a better teacher? This is a grand opportunity for you to show how you turned a negative into a positive.

FROM THE PRINCIPAL'S DESK:

One principal told me about a question she always asked: "Please share your personal feelings on winning and losing." She said she wanted to know how well a candidate could think on his or her feet as well as how the candidates were able to express themselves with a completely different mindset (from the usual teacher questions). She said she loved to hear responses such as "I like to win" or "I want my students to be winners in the classroom and in life." According to her, "Those responses showed that the candidate would do anything to ensure success in the classroom—they were candidates who would go the extra mile...above and beyond the usual expectations of teachers."

———————

#134: Tell me about a time when your co-operating teacher wasn't happy with your teaching.

A: During my first week of student teaching, I was very nervous and I jumped right into my math lessons without taking the time to do an anticipatory set. The students had puzzled looks on their faces, and I couldn't figure out why until my co-operating teacher pointed out that I'd left out one of the most important parts of any lesson. I realized how important it was to follow the standard lesson protocol and take the time to properly introduce every lesson. Since that first week, Mrs. Jesson has been very pleased with my performance.

This is not the time to blame others or to make lame excuses. Take full responsibility for your actions, and show how you were willing to make any necessary changes as a result of the incident. It is not necessary to go into a great deal of detail here; instead, point out a minor conflict and quickly explain how you used it to become a better teacher.

#135: Tell me about your most challenging discipline problem.

A: That would be Derek! Derek was unmotivated and didn't care about history; frankly, he couldn't have cared less about life in general. For Derek, everything was boring. In a conversation I had with him, I discovered that he loved stock cars. One day I brought in a photo of my brother's stock car and showed it to Derek. His face lit up like a Christmas tree! I arranged for Derek and my brother to meet after school one day, and the two of them couldn't stop talking for hours! From then on, I had his attention. He and I worked out a simple behavior plan—he'd do a certain amount of homework or a class assignment and in return he'd earn some points. The ultimate reward was the opportunity to work the pits at one of my brother's races. I never saw a student change so much as Derek. His final project for the course was on the history of stock car racing. It was phenomenal! Nobody had taken the time to find out what Derek was all about—but when we did he was a changed person.

You can almost "bet the farm" that you'll get asked one or two discipline-related questions. The interviewer wants to know how you handle one of the "constants" in the life of any classroom teacher. Provide a specific example, and show how you addressed the issue. Never talk in generalities on matters of discipline; demonstrate with specific details how you dealt with an issue.

INSIDER TIP

Before the interview, identify two or three specific discipline "problems" you encountered during student teaching. Write each of those out on an index card (don't use actual names), and detail how you handled each one in a positive way. Make sure that you don't over-emphasize the "negatives" of the situation, but rather focus on the "positives" (what you learned, how the student(s) improved, etc.). Keep those cards with you, and review them periodically before any scheduled interview.

#136: Who's the toughest professor you've ever had, and why?

A: There's no question—that would be Dr. Sutherland. I took three methods courses from him, and he always asked hard questions. He never asked easy or factual questions; he always pushed me mentally, always made me think outside the box. He was never satisfied with a simple answer—he always wanted an explanation or a personal opinion. I probably thought more in his classes than in all my other classes combined. But you know what? I became a better question-asker with my students as a result of his probing and pushing. He was tough, but he was also a good model!

Here's a delightful opportunity to put a positive spin on one of your challenges. Don't make the mistake of tearing someone down. You'll never win a friend with the interviewer if you do. Use this question as a chance to show how you are continuing to grow as both a teacher and as a person.

FROM THE PRINCIPAL'S DESK:

"One candidate made the mistake of bad-mouthing a particular professor who (according to the candidate) 'raised a major stink when he caught us text messaging during one of his god-awful-boring lectures!' What the candidate didn't realize was that the professor was my brother."

#137: What is your greatest weakness?

A: People sometimes tell me that I come up with too many creative ideas. I'm always trying to think "outside the box" when I design lesson plans, units, or extended projects. I always want to include more activities and projects in my lessons, and sometimes get impatient when I don't have enough time to do them all. I'm still learning how to be more patient with my creativity.

This is one of the best questions in any interview—for both the interviewer and the respondent. Always be ready for this one! This is not the time to rant about your imperfections or, even worse, those of others. Don't admit to a weakness in teaching a particular subject, in classroom management, or disciplining students. Select one or two personality attributes that are more general than specific. For example, being a perfectionist, running out of time, or not getting to everything on a "To Do" list. These are "imperfections" we all wrestle with. This is the only time you don't want to be too specific. Select an "innocent" weakness, and frame it in positive terms. Above all, keep your response short and sweet.

#138: Why weren't your grades better?

A: I had a great educational experience. I learned a lot while in college—not only about the art of teaching, but also about myself. I learned that if you want to succeed you need to devote yourself 100 percent all the time. When I first got to college, I was overwhelmed by all the requirements, the responsibilities, and the activities on and off campus. I got involved in lots of clubs, organizations, and extra-curricular activities. As a result, my grades suffered during my first two years. It was only when I was enrolled in my teacher-preparation courses that I realized that I would need to buckle down and commit myself 100 percent to my chosen profession.

Whatever you do, don't make excuses when answering this question. Take responsibility for your actions (or inactions). Don't try to bluff your way out of this question; the interviewer probably has seen your transcript and knows exactly what your GPA is. Own up to your mistakes, and show how you have grown as a result. Never get defensive or place blame.

FROM THE PRINCIPAL'S DESK:

"When asked a question regarding GPA and education courses, a candidate responded as follows: 'I learned the hard way not to schedule a class for Fridays at 3:00—too close to Happy Hour.' Needless to say, I didn't hire him."

#139: Why did you decide to major in biology (or history or elementary education)?

A: Ever since I was in fifth grade, I've been fascinated with biology. I've always had a desire to know as much as I can about the flora and fauna of a particular area. I belong to the local chapter of the Isaac Walton League, I've worked at the state natural history museum as a summer intern, and I established a pond study project while I was in high school. Biology is a love of mine, and I can't think of anything I'd rather do than share my passion for the subject with a new generation of learners.

This is an excellent opportunity to demonstrate your passion and ardor for a subject. Let the interviewer hear that excitement in your response; let him or her get a sense of how committed and sincere your interest is. Make sure you defend your choice of major with some specific examples of how you have used it outside of normal academic requirements (e.g., volunteer work; clubs, organizations, and community agencies; or out-of-classroom experiences). You'll earn major "brownie points" if you can show that your selection of a major was not one of convenience, but rather one of commitment.

#140: What do you think is the biggest challenge teachers face today?

A: Teachers are challenged from all sides—the media, parents, government officials, elected leaders, and communities. We are in the spotlight constantly. One of the greatest challenges we face is that of assessment. Are students learning to the best of their potential, and are teachers providing their students with the best-quality education possible? Educational initiatives such as "No Child Left Behind" and "Race to the Top" have put educational assessment on the front burner of educational reform. Are we teaching what we should be teaching, and are students achieving as they should be achieving? During my student teaching experience, I was able to fully integrate assessment throughout all my lesson plans—from beginning to end. For that, I can thank Dr. Cranshaw, who showed me how to effectively integrate assessment throughout any lesson or unit. I don't have all the answers regarding assessment, but I've had some excellent training and experiences I can use throughout my career.

Rule #1: Be sure you are up to date on the latest educational theories, initiatives, and issues. You will, sometime during the interview, be asked about your opinion or your experience in dealing with one of these concerns. Be sure to demonstrate how you have addressed an element of that issue sometime in your pre-service training. If you don't, you will be sending a very powerful message to the interviewer that you don't stay up to date and that you are unaware of what is happening outside the classroom. This is a mistake you can't afford to make.

#141: Why shouldn't we hire you?

A: You might not want to hire me because I'm young and inexperienced. But please don't let my youth and inexperience fool you. I assume you are looking for a teacher who will be a positive influence in the lives of students, who knows her craft, who can motivate students, and who can solve problems both big and small. I assume you are looking for someone with lots of classroom experience, lots of practical ideas, and lots of background knowledge about learning styles and teaching strategies. I believe I can bring all those attributes to this job. In student teaching, I worked closely with the other fifth-grade teachers to improve reading scores by 18 percent. I also was part of a team that initiated a behavior-intervention program with the school counselor. And I helped write a series of inquiry-based thematic units for the science program. I honestly believe you should hire me because I'm a go-getter and I'm intensely passionate about teaching.

This is a question that pops up every so often; it is designed to see if the candidate can think quickly on his or her feet. It's also asked to see if there is any negativity in the candidate's philosophy. The best way to answer is to turn the question around. Rather than focus on the negative, emphasize the positive instead. Notice how the response above was turned into a positive one that focused directly on what the candidate could bring to the school. Specific examples and experiences were used to support her philosophy with a very positive attitude.

#142: If you could change anything about your teacher-preparation program, what would it be?

A: I wish we would have more field experience hours required in preparation for student teaching. At High Tuition College, we were required to complete 150 hours of field experience prior to student teaching. I've always felt that that simply wasn't enough to prepare us for the demands and challenges of the student teaching experience. So, on top of that requirement, I spent a lot of time over breaks and vacations volunteering at my local elementary school. I was a guest reader in the school library for the "Readers are Leaders" club, I helped out with the after-school tutoring program, and I coached the junior soccer team. I wanted to obtain as many experiences with youngsters as possible, even beyond what the college required. I knew that those experiences would help me be a better teacher.

Don't bad-mouth your college or university teacher-training program (the interviewer may have graduated from there, too). Briefly mention one small aspect of the program that may not have met your expectations. Show how you dealt with that aspect in a positive way, going above and beyond the usual requirements to learn more than was required. This is a great chance to demonstrate how one of your strengths was used to address a problem or recurring situation.

> **✔EXTRA CREDIT**
>
> Talk with one or two of your college professors, and ask them to cite an area or two that they think needs some improvement or changing in the teacher-preparation program. Ask them to suggest what they might do to make that part of the program better. Consider their response(s) as part of your answer to the question above.

#143: What was your second career choice?

A: I've never considered anything else but teaching. I've been influenced by many teachers in my life—from elementary school all the way through college. I know how one teacher can change the life of a student. Perhaps I was that average student pushed to excel by Mrs. McDonald in sixth grade, challenged to go above and beyond by Mr. Donahoe in tenth grade, and inspired to create a "hands-on, minds-on" curriculum by Dr. Oliver in college. Teachers have had a profound influence in my life, and I would like to make that kind of difference in the lives of my students. I can't think of any other profession, or any other occupation, that would give me the opportunity to change lives in such a positive way as teaching. For me, there is no second career. I want to teach!

Don't even think about suggesting an alternate career path. This is when you must convince the interviewer—beyond a shadow of a doubt—that your life's mission is teaching. Demonstrate your overwhelming passion for the field, and let it be clear that teaching is in your blood, is an integral part of who you are, and is the singular pursuit of your life. This is not the time to be wishy-washy. Be clear, passionate, and compelling about your career choice.

#144: Describe a situation in which you made a difference in a child's life.

A: Karen was one of the students in Mrs. Ginnodo's fourth-grade classroom. I had been assigned there in order to complete some of my field experience hours. Karen had been through a succession of foster homes, didn't have a father, and barely knew anything about her mother. She had two dresses that she alternated wearing from day to day. She had seen tough times, and likely would continue to do so. But, for some reason, she and I connected. I have always enjoyed horseback riding, and Karen was a fan of horses. So I hunted up some horse books in the school library, and we read them together. We talked about horses, made models of horses, wrote horse stories together, created a PowerPoint presentation on horses, and even visited a friend's horse farm one Saturday morning. Probably, for the first time in her life, she smiled. And, probably, for the first time in her life, someone took the time to learn something about her. One of my professors always talks about the power of the affect in education. I got an opportunity to see that power in action…and I'll never forget it!

I particularly like this question. It provides an insight into the real educational philosophy of a candidate that goes beyond book learning and memorized strategies. It allows me to see into the true character of a person and whether his or her commitment to teaching is sincere and passionate. In short, are they in it for more than just a job? You would be well-served to practice this question (and your response). Of course, this is not the time to pontificate ("If it wasn't for me, she would never have…."), but rather be humble. Focus on the affective side of teaching, and let the interviewer know that you have been touched by students as much as you have by your own teachers and professors.

#145: Describe the best teacher you ever had and what he or she taught you about teaching.

A: That would be Mr. Hart, my 11th-grade English teacher. He was tough, demanding, challenging, and uncompromising. He never took second best—we had to turn in our best work, or it would come back to us with "Do Over" penned across the front. We probably had more to say about Mr. Hart—unflattering, to be sure—than any other teacher we had. But, as I look back, he taught me more about writing than anyone else. He taught me that writing is a subject of exactness, a subject of details and definitions. "You can't be mushy," he would say. He pushed us to new heights, prodded us into new and often uncomfortable areas, and made us all better writers. One of the primary reasons I want to be an English teacher is because Mr. Hart took an average student like me and turned her into a far better writer than she would have been otherwise. I want to make that difference in students' lives, too!

Most of us have been positively influenced by one or more teachers. We get into teaching because some teacher made a profound difference in our lives. Let the interviewer know how this person made a difference in your life and how you want to "pass the baton" to a new generation of learners. This is the time to be passionate, sincere, and complimentary. Like you, I've had a few really tough teachers in my life, but they planted some powerful seeds that have taken root and sprouted in each and every class I teach today. Make sure the interviewer knows precisely how you've been influenced and how you will influence others.

#146: How would you handle a student saying, "You are the worst teacher ever! I hate you!"

A: I would remember to focus on the behavior rather than on the student. I might say something like, "It seems as though you are upset with me. Would you care to explain further?" When teachers get comments like that, the worst response would be to put the student on the spot. Instead, a conversation is more productive when the emphasis shifts to the actual comment rather than the student's personality. I've also discovered that sending an "I message" is a very productive way of diffusing the student's anger, with a message such as "I understand that you are upset with me. I wonder if you can tell me why." To build up the trust necessary for an effective conversation, it's valuable to let the student vent and then get to the heart of the anger without assaulting the student's emotions.

This kind of question is a test of your discipline and classroom-management philosophy. Demonstrate that you are up on the latest behavioral strategies and techniques for handling student issues. If you were to say something like "I'd make the student go stand in the corner for ten minutes," you would clearly show that you do not have the student's best interests in mind or that you were not aware of appropriate behavior-management techniques. Make sure you can cite a specific technique (by name) and how you would apply it to a specific situation.

#147: What do you want your students to remember about your classroom?

A: I want students to remember my classroom as a comfortable place that supported their needs, both physically and psychologically, and in which each student felt secure and respected. I want my students to know that the classroom is their place; that it's not just the teacher's place into which they have been temporarily invited. I want them to know that the classroom invites student engagement and celebrates the work of all students. I want them to have a sense of ownership in the classroom, a sense that this is a place that supports, encourages, and respects each and every individual as a unique and contributing member of the class. I want them to believe that their "investment of self" in the classroom will pay off in incredible educational dividends and lifelong emotional growth.

This is another question that taps into your philosophy of education. That is to say, are you child-centered, or are you subject-centered? Do you place students ahead of standards, curriculum, and rules, or is it the other way around? Keep your response to this question focused on students, and you'll always score points.

FROM THE PRINCIPAL'S DESK:

"I am always impressed with candidates who have a 'children first' orientation with compassion and a missionary mindset."

#148:   If an administrator visited your classroom, what would he or she see?

A: She would see an educational environment in which every student is respected, trusted, and learning. She would see an active classroom where students are never absorbing information passively, but are, instead, actively participating in a curriculum that puts a premium on personal and meaningful engagement. She would see students taking responsibility for their learning through self-established goals, with projects and activities that are pedagogically sound and standards-based. She would see students achieving and challenged through higher-level-thinking questions, specific RTI activities, and a teacher dedicated to success. She would see a classroom that embraces every student's cognitive and affective potential. She would see a community of learners!

The answer to this question should focus, not on the physical environment, but rather on your philosophy of education. This is a question that gets to the heart of what it means to be a teacher. Here's where you can let your beliefs and your values shine. But be careful—this is not the time to ramble. Be concise, and keep your answer to two minutes or less.

#149:   If you are not successful in getting a full-time job, what will you do?

A: I am committed to teaching and education. Being a teacher is my top professional goal. I believe I can make a very positive contribution to this field, and I'm willing to wait for the right opportunity to make that happen. If it's not a full-time position, then I would be equally happy to be listed on any number of substitute teaching lists. The more opportunities I have to expand and improve my teaching abilities will be beneficial to my long-term goals. If I don't get that full-time job, I'll work harder, volunteer more, and take any opportunity I can to work with youngsters. This is what I want to do, and I'll take advantage of every opportunity possible to do it.

Don't be shy! Share your passion for teaching and your commitment to education. It's important that the interviewer knows of your universal desire to teach, your intense and dedicated drive to make a difference in the lives of children. That commitment must show through, just as much for a full-time teaching position as for a place on the substitute teaching list. By demonstrating that universal desire, you provide the interviewer with both reason and rationale for any and all positions in the school or in the district.

CHAPTER 9

HYPOTHETICAL AND SITUATIONAL SCENARIOS

What would you do if one of your students stood up and threw a book at you in the middle of a social studies lesson? Many teacher interviews include situational or hypothetical questions that test your ability to think on your feet and apply your teaching philosophy to a real-life event. Let's be honest—these are challenging simply because it is difficult to prepare for any single situation. Quite often, the question asked may be an isolated event or situation that recently occurred in the school. I recall an interview many years ago when the interviewer, completely out of the blue, asked me, "What would you do if you caught two of your male students in a sexual encounter in the bathroom?" As you might imagine, it was not a question I had anticipated, nor was it one I had prepared for. I recall stumbling my way through a response that seemed to satisfy the interviewer; yet I could only think the question was asked as a result of a recent incident. Yes, it caught me off guard, but I had practiced with other "hypotheticals" prior to the interview. (Incidentally, I was offered the job.)

INSIDER TIP

In a recent survey of teacher candidates around the country, it was reported that 38 percent of them were asked to respond to hypothetical or situational questions during an interview. Only about 20 percent of the candidates had rehearsed or prepared for those questions in advance of their interviews.

In the preceding chapters, I have presented you with 149 questions that principals and other hiring officers across the country regularly ask candidates for teaching positions in their schools, and I've provided you with surefire answers that, when molded to fit your experiences and educational views, will give these interviewers a positive view of your suitability to the job. In this chapter, I offer a bonus: additional questions of this situational type.

It seems reasonable to expect that you will get one or more situational or hypothetical questions during the course of an interview. It's important to remember that there are no absolutely perfect answers to these questions—there are differences of opinion, different philosophies, and different strategies used, depending on experience and background. In short, no two people will give the same answer to these queries. What is more important is that, quite often, these kinds of questions are asked to gauge three things:

1. **Your problem-solving abilities.** Every day, teachers are faced with situations and events for which there are no easy answers and for which they may not have received training. A student has an epileptic seizure in your classroom, a parent walks into your classroom swearing at you about his child's report card, a student steals money from your purse—these are all events that will test your problem-solving abilities...and your patience. If you can solve problems quickly in an often stressful interview situation, then it is likely you will be able to solve them in the classroom.

2. **Your poise.** Do you get flustered when presented with a new situation? Can you handle unexpected stress? Interviewers want to know how composed and how rational you will be in the often chaotic world of classroom teaching. Can you maintain a calm, collected demeanor, or will you "fly off the handle" at the slightest disruption?

FROM THE PRINCIPAL'S DESK:

"We once had a candidate who said, 'Excuse me,' got up at the start of the interview, got in his car, and drove away."

3. **Your general views about sound educational practices.** Are you aware of some of the common ways of handling discipline or maintaining classroom order? Do you know some of the "best practices" that differentiate the average teacher from the superior teacher? Are you comfortable with the principles and practices of child or adolescent psychology and their application in a classroom environment? While you may not be able to provide a perfect answer to a situational event, you should, at least, be comfortable with current research, practices, and principles regarding human nature and child development to formulate an appropriate response.

Responding to Hypotheticals

When presented with these problematic situations, there are several ways you can respond. I suggest you consider (and practice) the following.

Wait Time

You may be familiar with the teaching technique known as *Wait Time*. This is when you (as a teacher) allow students approximately five seconds of thinking time after asking them a question, which allows them to formulate an appropriate response instead of saying the first thing that strikes them. Teacher candidates who use *Wait Time* come across as thoughtful, rather than impulsive. Using those brief seconds can be a real asset in your ability to formulate a response. Equally important, it lets the interviewer know that you are not given to snap decisions or impulsive conclusions.

Q: **What would you do if a parent burst into your classroom yelling and screaming?**

A: [pause for a few seconds] I would first try to escort the parent outside. Closing the door to my room, I would allow the parent to vent his or her frustration or anger. I would never raise my voice or show any type of disrespect. I would permit the parent to vent for a minute or two and then try to calmly reason with him or her. Using direct eye contact and lots of "I" messages, I would try to arrive at the source of the anger. Knowing I had students waiting for my return to the classroom, I might ask for a conference after school or the opportunity to talk on the telephone. I would never demean the parents or assign any blame.

INSIDER TIP

It's mentioned elsewhere in the book, but it bears repeating: Ideal answers are from 30 seconds to two minutes. No more! No less!

Using Anecdotes

Use an anecdote. One of the best ways to respond to a hypothetical situation is to inject a story or anecdote about something similar that may have happened to you. Anecdotes have the added benefit of letting the interviewer know that you have had real-life experiences beyond the college classroom—experiences in student teaching, your field experience hours, or any volunteer work you may have done. This is a unique opportunity to demonstrate the wide variety of experiences you have had during your pre-service training. Whenever possible, use a story to underscore your experiences with students in several different situations.

Q: **What would you do if two of your students were fighting on the playground?**

A: The first thing I would remember is that nobody is "right" and nobody is "wrong." In fact, this happened one day during my student teaching experience. Two girls were fighting near the jungle gym. I quickly stepped in and separated them and gave them both an opportunity to sit down—apart from each other—and cool off. I then approached each one separately and asked her to share what happened and listened carefully. I didn't want to criticize either one, but wanted to give them a chance to get something off their chests and get to the reason for their disagreement.

Using Research

Cite a piece of research, refer to a professional organization, or relate a "best practices" technique. Let the interviewer know you are well-versed in the most relevant data and "book knowledge." By the same token, it would be equally important to demonstrate how you might put that knowledge into practice in a classroom situation.

Q: **What would you do with a class full of students who were totally turned off by science?**

A: The National Science Teachers Association has, for a number of years, been promoting an inquiry-based approach to science education, which encourages students to generate their own questions and then to discover the answers to those questions. One of the ways teachers can effectively use this approach to science education is through the 5-E Model of science education. During my student teaching experience in a fourth-grade classroom, I was able to develop several lessons using the 5-E Model—and I discovered some remarkable changes taking place in my students' attitudes.

Student Needs

Demonstrate that you always put the needs of your students first. Don't make the mistake of using a situational question as an opportunity to cast blame on the students you taught during student teaching ("I know I'm a much better teacher; however, I really got a lousy group of seventh graders in student teaching."). You'll essentially be shooting yourself in the foot. Use this opportunity to demonstrate that you will do everything possible to support, encourage, and build up your students. This is a chance for you to let an interviewer know that you are student-centered and student-directed. Anything less, and you can just let yourself out the door.

Q: **How would you deal with a difficult student, one who never did any work?**

A: Students are often unmotivated. My experience has been that many students don't try new things because they're afraid of failure. I believe that, as classroom teachers, we must establish and promote conditions that will emphasize and support an expectation of success for every student. I want every student to be successful, and so I need to tailor my instruction to make that happen. I'm a big fan of differentiated instruction because it shows a respect for the different ability levels in my classroom and for each student's ability to succeed. By adjusting my instruction for that unmotivated student, I believe I can make the needed connection for him or her.

✔**EXTRA CREDIT**

Never memorize "canned answers" to interview questions, including the answers in this book. Doing so will make you appear less than honest and certainly less believable. Personalize the answers, flavor them with your unique personality, spice them up with selected anecdotes...but never memorize them!

Common Hypothetical and Situational Scenarios

While it would be impossible to prepare for every scenario that might be posed in an interview, you can get a head start by practicing with several different scenarios. Find a friend or a classmate, and ask him or her to randomly select one or more hypothetical situations and pose the question(s) to you. Form a study group of several other individuals preparing for interviews, and pose hypothetical questions back and forth to each other. I strongly suggest that you make these practice sessions a regular part of your interview preparation.

The list that follows provides you with some "problematic" questions you may be asked in an interview. Please note this is not a finite list; however, by practicing with these questions and with the suggested response strategies outlined above, you should be very comfortable in answering almost any unexpected question.

- What would you do if you caught a student cheating on a test?

- How would you handle a parent who became very angry during a parent-teacher conference?

- What would you do if you discovered that one of your students was being physically, emotionally, or sexually abused?

- How would you deal with a violent or verbally abusive student?

- What would you do about a student who never did his or her homework?

- A student tells you his or her parents are getting divorced. What do you say?

- You catch a student smoking in the bathroom. What do you do?

- You know a certain student plagiarized a written report. How do you handle the situation?

- How would you handle a student who is verbally abusive to other students?

✔EXTRA CREDIT

Before any interview, write out a specific discipline plan for your classroom. Review notes from your courses, and read related resource books. Count on being asked one or more discipline-related questions.

- After you give an assignment, you notice a student sleeping at his or her desk. How do you handle this?

- A student is texting on his or her cell phone while you are lecturing. What would you do?

- Two of your students are fighting in the cafeteria. How would you deal with this situation?

- A student refuses to salute the flag during morning announcement. Tell me how you would handle this situation.

- You think the school's discipline policy is too lax or too easy. What would you say to the principal?

- One of your students, in a fit of anger, slaps your face. What's the first thing you would do?

- Over a period of several weeks, you notice more than one occasion when money is missing from your purse. What do you say to the class?

- A student falls off the monkey bars on the playground. What are some of the steps you would take?

- You are certain one of your colleagues is an incompetent teacher. How would you deal with that individual?

- One of your students absolutely hates math. What do you do to motivate him or her?

- A lesson absolutely "bombs" while the principal is observing you. What do you do?

INSIDER TIP

Hypothetical and situational questions will typically fall into one of two categories: 1) confrontational (angry parent, disruptive student) or 2) discipline/classroom management-related (inappropriate behavior, cheating).

You can count on dealing with one or more hypothetical situations during an interview. What you can't count on is the exact situation(s) an interviewer will pose. However, by regularly practicing with the sample situations in this chapter, and with the suggested types of responses, you will feel comfortably ready to respond to anything thrown your way.

CHAPTER 10

QUESTIONS *YOU* SHOULD ASK (AND QUESTIONS YOU *SHOULDN'T*)

Most professional interviewers will tell you that a good interview is a two-way street; interviews that get applicants jobs are those in which both participants contribute to the interview. If the interviewer does all the work, then the interview will be decidedly one-sided. Make some contributions! The interviewer has a limited amount of time and wants to know as much about you as possible, but doesn't necessarily want to do all the work.

In most interviews, you are given a golden opportunity to provide the interviewer with some valuable inside information. These are the times when you are offered the chance to ask your own questions. Don't blow this opportunity—more than one job has been won simply because the candidate showed a real interest in the school or the district through carefully crafted questions. These questions can reveal as much about your interest, desire, and motivation as they can in showcasing your talents and skills, particularly those talents that mesh with the school's philosophy.

It is always advisable to prepare a set of questions well before the interview. I suggest recording individual questions on separate index cards. Put the questions in priority order, or arrange them according to the categories below. Review the questions several times in advance of every interview. Be sure each question is specific; don't compose a generic set of questions for all your interviews, but rather make up a separate set of questions for each individual interview.

> ## INSIDER TIP
>
> Put your set of index cards in a pocket or in your purse, in a place where you can reach them very quickly and easily. Although you will know the questions on the cards, it is a good idea to read a question directly from a card. The set of prepared questions will always impress an interviewer, letting him or her know that you came to the interview well-prepared. In short, you did your homework.

Although most interviewers will frequently ask if you have any questions at the end of the interview, it is always advisable to sprinkle your questions throughout the interview. Again, this promotes the concept that a good interview is part of a shared responsibility, part of a give-and-take process, part of an evolving partnership. By knowing your questions ahead of time (and putting them in priority order), you will have some idea as to when you can use them during the course of the interview.

Asking your own questions also provides you with an opportunity to be pro-active rather than passive. They help underscore your sincere interest in building a working partnership, in becoming an active member of the school team. Of course, you don't want to take over the interview, but a relevant question here and there in the interview helps you highlight your strengths and how those strengths can be used effectively in the school.

> ## ✔EXTRA CREDIT
>
> Prepare a set of 15–20 questions you would like to ask in an interview. Plan on asking three to five carefully chosen questions throughout the length of the interview. Know your questions, and know when it would be appropriate to ask each one.

The key is not to wait until an interviewer asks you, "Do you have any questions?" That will make your interview like every other interview. Rather, plan your questions and when you want to ask them. You want to show initiative, and you want the interviewer to know that you are interested in the school or the district and not just a job. In many cases, those three to five questions may make all the difference in whether you get a teaching position.

A. Questions About the School/District

Let's assume you have researched the school/district via their Web site in the days prior to the interview. You've gathered information about their location, mission statement, physical facilities, sports teams, and philosophies. Perhaps you had the opportunity to talk to or communicate with some of the teachers or staff. You may have even been able to make a pre-interview visit to scope out the school grounds, watch the interactions between staff members, or visit one or two classrooms. All of that "homework" is valuable simply because it gives you a "feel" for the philosophy of the school, the atmosphere, and its day-to-day operation.

Equally important is the fact that all of that preliminary work will help you craft questions specific to that particular school. Instead of asking, "How is the cross country team doing this year?" (which could be used for any school) you might ask, "I see the cross country team has had some tough meets this year. As a former long-distance runner I'd like to contribute my expertise. What kinds of coaching opportunities in cross country or track would Lumberjack High School have?" Such a question would be specific to the school with whom you are interviewing.

FROM THE PRINCIPAL'S DESK:

"Don't ever ask a direct question of a certain individual sitting on a hiring panel. It puts the person on the spot."

This is not the time to ask questions that can be easily accessed via the Internet or through school or district publications. By asking such questions, you reveal that you haven't done your homework and you waste valuable interview time that could be better spent on other issues. Here are some appropriate questions to consider:

- What would you say are some of the strengths of this school/district?

- What are some of the challenges you anticipate in the next five years?

- I'm very student-oriented. Would you please describe the student body in more detail?

- What are some of the ways in which parents participate in school activities?

- You mentioned [a curriculum initiative] a few minutes ago. Could you tell me a little more about this?

- What new academic programs or extracurricular activities are being considered for the coming year?

- What are some of the support services for students?

- How is the curriculum aligned with state or national standards?

- What are some of your long-term goals for the school? For teachers?

- What do you see as some of your most pressing challenges in the coming year?

B. Questions About the Job/Position

Plan to ask one or two questions specifically about the position you are interviewing for. These questions should be designed to obtain more information about the specific responsibilities of the position as well as the day-to-day activities you would be expected to perform. This is a perfect opportunity to ask questions that will open the door on how you will be able to answer the single-most important question (see Chapter 6).

✔**EXTRA CREDIT**

Don't ask questions with "yes/no" answers ("Do you have a teacher-mentor program?"). It's important for you to pose questions allowing the interviewer an extended response—and you a chance to show how you can positively contribute to that situation.

- Could you please describe your teacher-mentor program?

- I noticed that the school is departmentalized. What do you see as some of the advantages of that organization?

- What types of opportunities are there for team teaching?

- How would you describe parent expectations for students? For teachers?

- I'm very interested in building my skills as a teacher. What staff-development opportunities are offered?

- What are some of the challenges you're experiencing in the reading program (or any other curriculum area)?

- What types of responsibilities outside the classroom are teachers expected to do?

- What do you see as some of the opportunities for community involvement?

- In what ways does the school/district support or encourage graduate work?

- How did this position open up?

FROM THE PRINCIPAL'S DESK:

"One of the best questions a candidate can ask in an interview is 'What opportunities for professional development can the district offer me?'"

C. Questions About the Teaching Environment

You want to know who you will be working with, some of the training opportunities provided to teachers, and how you can contribute to the overall program. While your focus in this section will be on those factors that take place during regular school hours, you also want to take this opportunity to demonstrate an interest in after-school contributions. Consider the following as possibilities:

- In what ways do parents get involved with the school? How would you like teachers to promote parent participation?

- What kinds of outreach or community-based initiatives have been implemented in the school in recent years?

- What are some new innovations or programs recently implemented (for your grade level or subject areas)? What kind of success have you had with these programs?

- How successful is your current discipline policy? What changes or modifications would you like to see?

- What are some of the club, extra-curricular, or coaching opportunities for teachers?

- What do you see as some of the major issues the school will need to address in the coming year? How would you like teachers to contribute to those challenges?

- What computer or technological resources are available for first-year teachers?

- I'm very interested in being part of a strong teaching team. In what ways do teachers get together—either during or after school hours—to build that teamwork?

D. Questions That Highlight Your Qualifications

INSIDER TIP

Always include one or two questions that showcase how your special qualifications or abilities can be a match for the school's or district's needs. While framed as questions, these are incredible opportunities to underscore the talents you (and only you) can bring to the school.

The primary purpose of these questions is to show how you and the school are a match; that is to say, that you have skills and talents that can make a specific and positive contribution to the welfare of the school and the welfare of the students in that school. If you've done your pre-interview homework, you'll be aware of some of the issues or concerns the school may have and how you might be able to address those concerns. These questions will also help you promote your enthusiasm and interest in the position.

- I worked with kids on a number of after-school programs during my student teaching experience and thoroughly enjoyed them. What opportunities are there for me to continue those efforts here?

- I have good organizational and management skills. I've worked closely with our public library setting up summer reading programs and an active youth program. How might I contribute those skills to this school?

- I enjoy working with students after the regular day is over. What extracurricular academic programs are offered? Which ones would you like to see offered?

- Coaching is one of my passions, and I've been involved in youth volleyball programs. In what ways can I contribute my coaching experience to Snowy River Middle School?

- As I mentioned, I have a lot of training in piano. In what ways would it be possible for me to assist with the music program?

- I was a member of the Chess Club in college, and I've competed at the regional level. Chess has helped me be both an analytical and a critical thinker, and I'd like to contribute to that process here at Shady Glen Elementary School. What would be some of the possibilities?

E. Questions to Close the Interview

It is always to your advantage to sprinkle questions throughout the entire interview. That said, it is more than likely that the interviewer will end the interview by asking you if you have any final questions. This is not the time to bombard the interviewer with a dozen or more questions. It is, however, an excellent opportunity for you to "seal the deal" by posing one or two final questions. The questions you choose will depend on what you and the interviewer have discussed previously and the information you have shared about your qualifications and background.

Several interview experts suggest that this is the ideal time to ask when a decision will be made regarding the teaching position. Principals around the country seem to be divided on this point. Some told me that candidates demonstrate their sincere interest in the position by asking when a decision will be made, while other principals indicated that the question focuses too much on the candidate's needs rather than those of the school. Still, here are two suggested ways of asking the "decision question" while emphasizing your potential to the interviewer:

- I sincerely believe that I can make a most positive contribution to Wide Open Spaces Elementary School. I would love to bring my background and expertise in working with remedial readers, in local community literacy programs, and tutoring at the Salvation Army to the school's overall reading program. When do you anticipate making your decision on the position?

- I certainly share your concern about the decline in science achievement scores. I would hope that my student teaching experiences in the after-school Chemistry Club and my work with Professor Enzyme in judging local science fairs could be put to good use here at Stegosaurus High School. When would you hope to make a final decision?

Here are some other questions you may wish to consider near the conclusion of an interview:

- What is your proudest accomplishment (as a principal, as a school)?

- How might I be able to contribute to the success of the school?

- How can teachers (or students, or parents, or community members) make this a better school?

- Where would you like the social studies program to be in five years?

- What would you like students to remember most about this school (after they leave or after they graduate)?

- What one quality or attribute would you like to see in all your teachers?

- What makes this a good school? What would make it a better school?

INSIDER TIP

According to professional interviewer Tony Beshara, "If I have learned one thing since I got into this business, it is that the candidates who get the best jobs and make the best opportunities for themselves are the candidates who ask the best questions."

F. Questions You Shouldn't Even Think About Asking!!

Use the examples above, write them down, practice saying them out loud, and always have them at the ready to use at selected points in the discussion. But don't ask *any* of the following questions! If you do, you might as well pack up your bags and slip out the door, because you will have practically doomed your chances for any kind of job at that school. Trust me, the following questions—which I obtained directly from principals all across the country—are destined to make the principal's job just a little easier: They are guaranteed to eliminate you from any further consideration as a teacher candidate.

You'll quickly note that most of these questions are self-serving and self-involved. While some will be obvious "no-no's," others may appear to be less so. Nevertheless, please do yourself a tremendous favor and strike all of these from your interview preparations. By the way, all of these questions have been asked and are continuously being asked by teacher candidates. Not a single individual asking these questions was ever offered a teaching job!

- *How much will I be paid?"* Don't ask any questions related to salary or pay. If you are more interested in money than teaching, then you're in the wrong profession.

- *What kinds of benefits will I get?"* Questions about benefits are always considered inappropriate. After you get hired is the time to ask this question.

- *How long do you expect me (or teachers) to be at school each day?"* Stay away from any questions about school hours. Good teachers have no time clock.

- *Will I be able to take time off for personal business?"* Asking about time for personal business is never a good idea. It demonstrates your lack of commitment.

- *As a man, don't you think I should get some preferential treatment here?"* Don't be stupid enough to suggest anything remotely sexist. If the principal doesn't kick you out the door, I will!

- *How many black or Hispanic kids are in this school?"* It's none of your business to inquire about the community's ethnicity. Any suspected biases or prejudices, and you'll quickly be escorted back to the parking lot.

- *Do you celebrate Hanukah or Christmas here?"* Questions about a community's religious, political, or socio-economic breakdown are always in poor taste.

- *Will I be able to keep my part-time job at Wal-Mart?"* Do you really want to show that you are not totally committed to the teaching profession?

- *I heard that teachers have to do bus duty once a week. Is that true?"* Asking about ancillary duties will always get you in hot water.

- *Will I get in trouble if I punish a kid?"* Stay away from questions that might indicate any discomfort with discipline.

- *Do I have to join the teacher's union in this district?"* Questions about the "bargaining unit" are never appropriate. When you get hired you'll get all the relevant information.

- *Can I transfer to another grade after this year?"* Remember, you're applying for a specific job. Don't suggest that it's not your first priority.

When asked, these questions essentially "kill" any chances a candidate has in getting a teaching job. Don't even consider them!

CHAPTER 11

ILLEGAL QUESTIONS

From time to time you may be asked an illegal question. Fortunately, those times are rare, but they do occasionally occur. An illegal question is one that probes into your personal life, beliefs, or background. Federal law forbids employers from discriminating against any person on the basis of sex, age, race, national origin, or religion. Questions that delve into these areas are both inappropriate as well as illegal.

Most interviewers are aware of these questions, and it is indeed the rare occasion when you would be asked a question that is not directly related to the job. However, the interviewer may be new and not aware of the types of questions that can be asked and those that can't be asked. Perhaps he or she is trying to put you in a stressful situation to see how you would react (or over-react). Maybe the interviewer has a predetermined type of candidate in mind and is trying to find someone who matches those parameters without giving thought to the appropriateness of the questions. Or you may be asked inappropriate questions out of sheer ignorance. Although these occasions are uncommon, you need to consider how you might respond if you were asked an illegal question.

In consulting with administrators and professional interviewers around the country, I discovered that there are several schools of thought on this issue. These include the following:

1. You could tell the interviewer that the question is illegal and that you are not going to answer it. While you are certainly within your rights to make just such a response, it may have more negative consequences than you would like. Above all, your response would undoubtedly make the interviewer

uncomfortable and would, most certainly, give him or her a negative impression of you. In other words, you may be 100 percent right, but your response would be viewed as 100 percent wrong.

2. Another school of thought says that you should ignore the illegality of the question and just go ahead and answer it, because you are more interested in the teaching position than you are in the appropriateness of the question asked. In other words, you may decide that the job is much more important than the principle (or principal).

3. You can simply, respectfully, and politely decline to answer the question. A response such as "I'm somewhat uncomfortable with that question and would prefer not to answer it at this time" is suggested. The problem with this response—even though it is very appropriate—is that it may be seen as defensive and antagonistic, two qualities no principal wants to deal with. Even though the interviewer may be downright stupid to ask an illegal question, you don't want to compound that stupidity by pointing it out to him or her.

4. You could feign ignorance when asked an illegal question. That is, pretend that you aren't aware of the illegality of the question and, instead, ask for some clarification or explanation. For example, if you were asked, "What political party do you belong to?" you might respond as follows: "I'm not quite sure I understand what you're getting at. Could you please explain to me how my political affiliation might be related to my role as a tenth-grade Spanish teacher?" You've effectively told the interviewer that the question was illegal, and you've also effectively dealt with a stressful situation. Some interviewers might see this in a positive way, but others might take it as a personal "slap in the face." Unfortunately, you'll never know ahead of time.

While there is no hard-and-fast rule on how to deal with illegal questions, it is an issue you need to consider well in advance of any interview. Chances are slim that you will be presented with one of the questions in this chapter, but you need to keep in mind that you are now in a very tight race with a select group of individuals all competing for the same position. How you answer a single illegal question might "tip the scales in your favor," ultimately determining whether or not you are offered the job. In short, prepare for the worst, but give them your best.

After talking with elementary and secondary principals around the United States, most of them suggested that the most appropriate course of action is to turn what may be a negative situation into a positive response. Instead of giving a simple response ("I'm 37 years old!"), elaborate and provide the interviewer with additional information that demonstrates how that particular factor is an asset to your career as a classroom teacher.

Q: **How old are you?**

A: I'm 37 years old. In those 37 years, I've raised three children, volunteered at our local public library as a storyteller, worked for the Big Brother/Big Sister organization in town, and been a Cub Scout leader for my son's troop. I've had varied and diverse experiences with primary-level children and would hope to bring all those experiences to Pinedale Elementary School as a second-grade teacher.

✔**EXTRA CREDIT**

The key to answering an illegal question is to subtly shift the focus away from the easy one- or two-word answer and onto one of your strengths. Demonstrate how the "illegality" can be viewed as a positive quality, and you've effectively put out a fire, while demonstrating your spark.

Here are four other examples of illegal questions and how you might respond:

Q: **How long have you had that disability?**

A: I lost my finger when I was a young child helping my grandfather on his farm. I grew up in a rural environment, and I guess I've always enjoyed the outdoors. I'd like to be able to contribute my interest and fascination with flora and fauna with this new generation of learners. I've been fortunate to live most of my life hiking, exploring, and enjoying nature, and I believe I can help young people appreciate, and become part of, the natural world through an inquiry-based science curriculum—one that offers lots of outdoor experiences and takes advantage of their natural inquisitiveness about nature.

Q: **Do you plan to get pregnant?**

A: My husband and I have no immediate plans to have children, but you never know. We both love children and have always gotten a lot of pleasure working as camp counselors and in numerous after-school projects. I love opportunities where I can help youngsters become their best, realize their potential, and grow and learn as members of society. I guess I'm just passionate about children and look forward to the possibility of affecting their lives in as many positive ways as possible.

Q: **Where were you born?**

A: I was born in northern California. I grew up in the Bay Area and had the pleasure of attending schools that were ethnically diverse, racially mixed, and multicultural. I've eaten varied foods, celebrated interesting holidays, participated in several cultural traditions, and been to any number of religious ceremonies. I believe I can bring that diversity of experiences into my classroom to show children how we can all live together if we just take the time to learn about each other's customs, traditions, and beliefs. I want to give students the same kinds of experiences I was fortunate enough to have in my early years.

Q: **Are you divorced?**

A: My former husband and I separated a few years ago. We had separate goals in life. Mine was to be a teacher. Ever since I became the room mother for my son's first grade classroom, I've had a yearning to be a classroom teacher. I'm fascinated with how kids learn and especially with the ways that teachers can positively influence that learning. I've always had a burning desire to work with children—helping them grow, learn, and develop—and teaching seemed to be the most natural way to do that.

INSIDER TIP

You need to decide ahead of time how you might respond to an illegal question. What are you most comfortable with? What type of response will put you in the best light without giving away sensitive or unnecessary information? In short, how can you turn a negative situation into a positive one?

Following is a list of selected illegal questions. Take some time to practice how you might respond to several of these. As you review this list, you will quickly note that the bulk of these questions tend to be posed more to women than to men. This factor is as much a part of outdated stereotypes as it is of antiquated perceptions about the role of women in the workplace. Know that this bias is there, but also know that there are ways you can deal with it (whether male or female) that will help push those stereotypes out of the public consciousness and to the back pages of history books.

- When were you born?
- Are you married, divorced, separated, single, or gay?
- Do you attend church regularly?
- What illnesses kept you from student teaching this semester?
- Do you plan to get pregnant?
- Are you on the pill?
- How often do you see a doctor?

- Have you ever been diagnosed with ADHD?
- What do your parents do?
- How long have you had that disability?
- Have you ever been treated for depression?
- That's an interesting accent. What country are you from?
- Do you have any medical or psychiatric problems?
- Are you living with anyone?
- Where did your family come from?
- Have you ever sued an employer or co-worker?
- Have you ever declared bankruptcy?
- When are you planning to start a family?
- What political party do you belong to?
- What is your religion?
- Do you have many debts?
- Do you own or rent your home?
- Where were you born?
- Do you observe any religious holidays?
- How many children do you have? How old are they?
- How old are you?
- What branch of the military were you in? What kind of discharge were you given?
- What is your native language?
- What does your spouse think about your career choice?
- How much do you weigh?
- How tall are you?
- What kinds of political or religious organizations do you belong to?
- Have you ever filed a Worker's Compensation claim?
- What kind of insurance do you carry?
- Have you ever been arrested?

FROM THE PRINCIPAL'S DESK:

"I once made the mistake of asking a non-traditional candidate how old she was. She replied, 'These gray hairs are from raising three kids, coaching an after-school soccer program, teaching Sunday School for eleven years, and volunteering at the local library. That's experience you're seeing!' We both chuckled and had a great conversation for the rest of the interview. But I never asked that question again."

Believe it or not, an illegal question gives you a unique opportunity to demonstrate how your strengths and experiences can be used to impress an interviewer. With sufficient practice, you can effectively show how to turn a potential "negative" into a solid "positive."

CHAPTER 12

32 QUESTIONS TO ASK YOURSELF

Very few people get a job offer immediately after their first and only interview (myself included). You should treat each interview as a stepping stone, an experience that will prepare you better for subsequent interviews. No interview is perfect; each one has a few slips, bumps, or "hiccups" that can be smoothed out and improved. In short, there is no such thing as a perfect interview. You should look at each one as preparation for the ones to follow. As someone who has been on both sides of the desk many times, I can tell you that some interviews are better than others; but no single interview is perfect.

The successful interviewee views each interview as part of the "training program" for every other interview to follow. View the experience as a way to "train" for every other interview. Thus, it is critically important that you self-assess, that you evaluate your performance so that you can do better next time.

One of the best ways to accomplish that self-assessment is to ask yourself a series of questions immediately after any interview. My suggestion is that you ask yourself these questions within one hour after an interview has been completed. Pull into the back of a local shopping mall, go into a nearby coffee shop, or park at a fast-food restaurant. Take the time to record your thoughts, impressions, and reactions. Don't wait until you get home or back to the dorm; do it right away.

INSIDER TIP

Research shows that most people forget 80 percent of what they hear within 48 hours. If you want to recall the events of an interview, it's best to do it within the first hour after experiencing it.

As soon as the interview is over, record your impressions and reactions. Don't rely on memory. It is imperative that you ask yourself the questions below within minutes of the end of an interview. Jot down your first impressions and reactions; get all those thoughts down on a sheet of paper. The sooner you do this, the better you'll be able to evaluate the results.

✔**EXTRA CREDIT**

Have a note pad or legal pad in your car. Place the note paper on the driver's seat of your car before you walk into a school for a scheduled interview. It will be the first thing you see (and should use) when you get back into your car.

A. Questions to Ask Yourself About Your Strengths

- What are my professional/teaching strengths?

- What are my personal strengths?

- Did I show how my talents and skills are a match for the school/district? In what ways?

- What are two or three of the most important features of my background that will be benefits for this school or district?

- Are the things I think are important in my background the ones a principal will think are important?

- Was I able to clearly communicate myself and my benefits to the interviewer?

- What makes me unique? What are three or four of my most important features and benefits that make me a better candidate than my competitors?

B. Questions to Ask Yourself About Your Weaknesses

- Did I present my weaknesses in a positive light? Provide an example.

- Did I avoid being defensive about the mistakes I've made in the past? How did I turn them into positives?

- From this person's point of view, what are my most prominent weaknesses?

- How could I present them in subsequent interviews?

C. Questions to Ask Yourself About the Interviewer

- Did I make a "connection" with the interviewer? Provide an example.

- What were the most important things the interviewer was interested in discovering? Did I communicate those well enough?

- Did the interviewer like me personally?

- What aspects of my experience or background should I emphasize in a follow-up e-mail or letter to the interviewer?

D. Questions to Ask Yourself About the Position

- What seemed to be the two or three most important requirements of the teaching position?

- Can I teach at that grade level?

- In light of the job requirements, what are my most unique attributes?

- Was I clear about my unique features, advantages, and benefits?

E. Questions to Ask Yourself About the Overall Interview

- Was my presentation clear, concise, and smooth?

- What questions could I have answered better?

- What questions could I have asked that I didn't?

- Based on this interview, what are the risks in hiring me as a teacher?

- What can I do now to further my candidacy?

- Based on what I know and feel, will I be invited back for subsequent interviews?

- Do I know who else I will interview with next, if I am called back?

FROM THE PRINCIPAL'S DESK:

"I am most impressed with a candidate's ability to demonstrate and describe the passion they have for teaching."

F. Questions to Ask Myself About My Overall Performance on This Interview

On a scale of 1 (low) to 10 (high), how would I rate my overall performance in this interview:

1 2 3 4 5 6 7 8 9 10

On a scale of 1 to 10, what are my chances of moving up to the next stage in the interviewing process (if there is a next stage):

1 2 3 4 5 6 7 8 9 10

On a scale of 1 to 10, what is my chance of getting this teaching position:

1 2 3 4 5 6 7 8 9 10

- This is what I would change/improve in my next interview:

_____

_____

_____

_____

- This is what I would say or do again in my next interview:

_____

_____

_____

_____

- Summary Statement:

  _____

  _____

  _____

  _____

_____

Your honest appraisal of each interview will help you do that much better on each subsequent interview. Please don't neglect this valuable step in the interview process. Your self-assessment will make you a much more valuable candidate (and potential teacher) during this critical stage in your professional career.

CHAPTER 13

FOLLOW-UP AND FOLLOW-THROUGH

When I was in high school and college, I ran the mile as a member of the track team. I studied videos of some of the world's greatest middle-distance runners for training tips and race tactics. Far too many times, I saw middle-distance races lost in the last four or five yards because, as my high school coach used to say, "the guy didn't power through the tape." I watched as potential winners, seemingly in the lead with less than ten yards to go, slowed down a little to ease through the finish tape. It was in those final yards that they would get passed by another competitor, losing the race by mere inches simply because they relaxed just a little as they approached the finish line. As a runner I was trained to always imagine that the finish line was ten yards farther down the track than it actually was, so I never lost a race at the finish line.

The same can be said for interviews. Too many candidates think that the end of the interview is the end of the "race." It's not. The job search process doesn't end with the interview. It is still possible to positively and permanently influence the interviewer and tip the scales in your favor.

The Thank-You Letter

Here's a basic fact of life: Sending a thank-you letter won't guarantee you a job; but not sending one will certainly hurt your chances. According to at least one research study, only about 37 percent of all interviewees sent thank-you letters to interviewers.

When you consider that candidates at this stage of the process are so evenly matched, then it only stands to reason that some little thing—like a thank-you letter—can make all the difference in the world. This is a golden opportunity for you to make an impression and to differentiate yourself from the rest of the pack.

INSIDER TIP

A survey from CareerBuilder.com found that a significant number of hiring managers would not hire someone who did not send a thank-you letter after the interview.

Not only is this proper etiquette, it's also smart! It's a wonderful opportunity to sell *yourself* to the interviewer or the committee one more time. You might be the only one to do it, the only one who made the effort. And you might be the only one who gets the job offer!

Write the letter as soon as possible—within two hours of the interview, while details are still fresh in your mind. If you have previously corresponded with the interviewer via e-mail, it is appropriate to send your letter as an e-mail. If most of your correspondence has been through the regular mail system, then you should send your letter via "snail mail." Whatever method you select to send your letter, it is vitally important that the letter arrive before the final decision is made. If you wait a couple of days before sending the letter, you may have lost a beautiful opportunity to put an exclamation mark on the entire interview process.

INSIDER TIPS

- Do not text your thank-you letter!
- Only send your thank-you letter as an e-mail if you have received e-mails directly from the interviewer or principal.
- If you send a thank-you letter via e-mail, follow up by sending a hard copy of the letter through the regular postal system.

A thank-you letter should be brief, no more than one typewritten page (single-spaced), and specific to the individual and the school. Do not make the mistake of sending a form thank-you letter. Make sure it is personalized.

Your letter should be no more than three complete paragraphs. Here is what you must include:

- Express your appreciation for the opportunity to interview for the position in the school or with the district.

- Indicate your enthusiasm and passion for the position and for the school or district.

- Briefly recap one or two strengths and how they relate to the specifics of the teaching position or the school. This is also a wonderful opportunity, once again, to answer the question that is never asked (see Chapter 6).

- Clearly state:

  1. Your sincere appreciation for the interviewer's time;

  2. How you can be contacted if additional information or materials are needed; and

  3. That you look forward to a positive response.

All that may seem like a lot, but take a look at the two examples that follow and you'll see how all those crucial elements of a well-crafted thank-you letter can be integrated.

✔EXTRA CREDIT

Consider taking the time to make up some business cards that include your photo and contact information. It would be appropriate to clip one of those cards to your thank-you letter as a gentle reminder of who you are.

123 Main Street
Grand, PA 19876
April 23, 20XX

Mr. Noah Lott, Principal
Square Root Elementary School
1234 Mathematics Boulevard
Numerical, PA 17654

Dear Mr. Lott:

I thoroughly enjoyed meeting with you today about the fifth-grade position at Square Root Elementary School. Thank you for the time and opportunity to share how my qualifications might be appropriate for the unique challenges of this position.

I was particularly impressed with the school's commitment to a literature-based reading program. As we discussed during our conversation, during my student teaching experience at Once Upon a Time Elementary School I was part of a team of teachers that successfully introduced a literature-based program to the primary grades. I believe I can bring that same level of energy and commitment to the reading program at Square Root.

Again, many thanks for your time. I look forward to a positive review of my application and to the possibility of contributing my passion for teaching to Square Root. Should you require any additional information, please don't hesitate to contact me at (717) 555-1212 or pgturner@wannateach.com.

Respectfully,

Paige Turner

Paige Turner

987 Highway 133
Carbondale, CO 81623
May 12, 20XX

Dr. Hiam Smartt, Principal
Magnanimous High School
5678 Academic Lane
Denver, CO 80226

Dear Dr. Smartt:

Thank you for meeting with me today to discuss the position you have available for a tenth-grade biology teacher. I thoroughly enjoyed speaking with you.

I was particularly excited to learn about the school's commitment to community-based learning. As we discussed, I have been very involved in the Roaring Forks Valley community in helping to develop educational programs, environmental seminars, and "traveling trunks" for the Crystal River Conservancy as they seek to involve more students in their outreach efforts. I believe my experiences in local environmental education programs will allow me to make a positive contribution to the Biology Department's "Community Commitment" project.

Again, thanks ever so much for your time and for a most interesting interview. I look forward to hearing from you in the near future.

Sincerely,

Dusty Rhodes

Dusty Rhodes

FROM THE PRINCIPAL'S DESK:

"The thank-you letter is a way of gently reminding the interviewer of who you are and distinguishing yourself from the dozen or so applicants who might have been interviewed for the position."

The Secret Benefit of a Thank-You Letter

Sending a thank-you letter may seem old-fashioned and antiquated. It's not! It's simple common courtesy. Besides, a thank-you letter can make you stand out from other similarly qualified candidates. Thank-you letters have three major advantages:

1. The letter will be a reminder to the principal or interviewer of who you are and what you stand for.

2. If written correctly, the interviewer will (once again) see how your set of skills, abilities, and teaching prowess relate to the advertised position.

3. The letter will underscore your communication skills, desire to become part of an academic team, and enthusiasm for the position.

✔EXTRA CREDIT

If you have been interviewed by several interviewers (a panel interview, for example), don't just send a thank-you letter to the head interviewer. Send individualized thank-you letters to each person on the panel.

I was recently part of a six-person team interviewing candidates for a newly opened teaching position. One of the candidates sent an individual and personalized thank-you note to every member of the team within 24 hours. She was the one offered the job.

You may well be one of the few (or only) candidate(s) to send a thank-you letter after an interview. That single factor may be the one item that "seals the deal" in helping you get the teaching position of your dreams. Do it!

REALITY CHECK ✔

Let's face it—teaching is tough, and teaching interviews are also tough. Don't, for a minute, think that an interview is a casual walk through the park. Under the best of circumstances, it is a time when two individuals meet—one is trying to sell something, the other is trying to decide if he or she wants to buy it. And the stakes are enormous.

- The cost of hiring a brand-new classroom teacher is estimated to be approximately $75,000–$100,000, a figure that includes salary, benefits, training, health insurance, retirement fund, and other "extras" for one year.

- An average teacher will earn approximately $4.2 million dollars over the course of a 35-year career. That's quite an investment for a school district. As you might imagine, they want to be sure they get their money's worth.

INSIDER TIP

One of the biggest concerns any interviewer has is the fear of making a hiring mistake. Hiring mistakes cost time, money, and reputation—items no administrator can afford to lose.

When you are buying a new product, there are typically three things you want to know:

1. Will I like it?
2. Will it work properly?
3. How long will it last?

Those are the same questions an administrator wants to know about every candidate who interviews for a teaching position. Answer all three questions to the satisfaction of the interviewer, and you have a great shot at a job! Fail to answer any one of them, and you'll probably find yourself in a revolving series of seemingly endless interviews.

- The person who has the highest "likeability factor" is the one who, most likely, gets the job. Quite often, it's the person who can best "sell" himself or herself to the interviewer. Are you friendly, engaging, interesting to be with, and someone I would like to have on my team? Do I like you?

- You must be both competent and capable. Do you have intellectual and emotional skills to effectively teach young people? Can you manage instruction and a classroom? Are you aware of current issues and strategies, and how will they be part of your classroom environment?

- What can you do to contribute to the school/district? How do your unique talents serve the immediate and long-range needs of the school/district? Are you able to put the school's or district's needs first? Is there a match between your talents and the needs of the school?

Remember that teaching is about people. Textbooks, computers, pencils, journals, and Smart Boards are just some tools that can facilitate that human interaction and exchange of information we call education. All of your training will mean little if you don't take advantage of the ideas in this book, ideas from those who hire and have been hired. These are the strategies of interview success—*your interview success.*

The more you prepare, the better your chance for success. This is your big chance to *Ace Your Teacher Interview!* Don't blow it!

At this particular point in many business books on job-interview techniques and strategies, the author wishes you "good luck." I'm not going to do that! Getting a teaching position is not a matter of luck; it is not a matter of chance or fortune or circumstances beyond your control. This is not the lottery we are talking about here. This is real life!

This is your future; this is what you have been working for over the course of the past four or five years. Do you want to leave your future to the elements of chance or fortune or just plain luck? I hope not!

I do, however, wish you great success. That success will come from extended and sufficient preparation, homework, and practice. The more you invest in the interview, the more you will reap. This book has been written to give you an edge on the competition. I have seen what happens in "knock your socks off" interviews, those interviews in which a powerful synergy evolves between an interviewer and a candidate; those interviews in which the interviewer knows, long before the interview is over, that this is the person "we want in our school"; those interviews in which a brand-new teacher walks out with both confidence and a job offer.

You now have the tools to make that interview *your* interview!

INSIDER TIP

If you need some friendly advice, the answer to a specific interview question, or the latest (and greatest) tip, you can e-mail me once (afredericks60@comcast.net). I promise to respond to your first inquiry. So please save it for a time when you could really use the help.

And don't forget one last tip that could serve you well: There's a great blog that has lots of answers and resources for you, too—just go to http://aceyourteacherinterview. blogspot.com.

NONTRADITIONAL CANDIDATES—WHAT YOU NEED TO KNOW

Okay, so you're not 22 anymore, your hair may be thinning or graying or missing, you've got a couple of extra pounds where they shouldn't be, and you've been "around the block" a couple of times. You've had a job (or several jobs), you've had a child (or several children), and you've had a wrinkle (or several wrinkles) sneak into your facial features. You're mature, traveled, and sophisticated. You pay a mortgage, wash stacks of dirty dishes, shuffle kids between soccer practice and Scouts, do endless loads of laundry, fall asleep in front of the TV, and can't even remember the last time you had a "night out."

You're a nontraditional student!

Colleges of education (mine included) are seeing an influx of nontraditional students enter their classrooms. (The latest government figures indicate that about 36 percent of all college students are nontraditional students.) These are people who are looking for a second career, those who left college to raise a family and now want to get back into the work force, individuals who were laid off from other jobs and are now looking for something a little more meaningful in life, and working mothers whose kids are now in school and who want some career satisfaction and a couple of extra dollars in the family treasury. These are people who are older, wiser, and more experienced than the typical college student. Have I described you well?

Nontraditional students often have a different set of fears and apprehensions about interviews than "average" college students. They often feel that their age is an impediment to getting hired. Well, let's set the record straight on that! In my conversations with administrators around the country, my surveys of professional interviewers, and my own experiences in working with nontraditional students for more than a quarter-century, there are three critical points that give you, the non-traditional student, a distinct advantage in the hiring process.

1. Your age is an asset! Let me repeat that—**your age is an asset!** Because you have a couple of extra years under your belt, you also have more life experiences. In all likelihood you've traveled to other parts of the country or to foreign countries, you've read a wide array of books, visited a wide array of art galleries and museums, and enjoyed a wide array of restaurants. You've conversed with people from many cultures, many lands, many religions, and many beliefs—in short, you've seen life outside your community. Numerous principals have told me that all those experiences are what they want in a classroom—whether that classroom is an elementary one or a secondary one. All those experiences make you a more well-rounded individual and a much stronger teacher.

FROM THE PRINCIPAL'S DESK:
"Experience is the best teacher! I'll always take experience over a GPA."

2. You also have roots! In all likelihood, you have been living in proximity to the college or in the same neighborhood for several years. And, in all likelihood, you are planning to stay there for several years in the future. You have, most likely, established connections through your local church, temple, or synagogue; formed lasting friendships with people in one or more volunteer agencies; socialized with the parents of your children's friends; or made social connections with people in a former job or your own neighborhood. There's a good chance you're not planning to run off to Las Vegas with some "hunky" construction worker or join a commune of post-modern environmentalists in northern California. The fact that you have roots means you're going to stay around for a while, definitely a major advantage in the eyes of any school principal.

3. You know kids. You may have your own family. You've raised one or more kids—you've fed them at 2:00 in the morning; changed their diapers; got them their first pair of shoes; carpooled them to Little League; patched up their scrapes and bruises; shuttled them to an endless succession of athletic events, band practices, and pajama parties; and helped them chase snowflakes on the first snowfall of winter. You've comforted them when they were down and cheered them when they won a third-place ribbon in the Parade of Pets

in second grade. You're a parent, and you know kids! You know how kids operate, how they behave, and how they learn. You've had on-the-job training with children that cannot be duplicated by any college of education. You've been there and done that! Any principal (worth his or her salt) will tell you that that experience is priceless—absolutely priceless—for a future teacher.

INSIDER TIP

Please don't think for a minute—or even a second—that you are coming into a teacher interview with a set of deficits. You are coming in with two or three unique characteristics not possessed by the average candidate. These are advantages of the first order. These are assets any school would welcome. These are invaluable!

What You Need to Know

A job interview is much more than simply providing the correct responses to a set of questions. It is an opportunity for you to present yourself and for the principal or interviewing committee to see who you are as a person and who you will be as a teacher. An interview is a wonderful opportunity for you, the nontraditional student, to exhibit your unique experiences in concert with the mission of the school. Here are ten tips to help you in that process:

1. **Focus on your "can-do" attitude.** As a nontraditional student, you've probably been in the work force, including the home-work force. You know how to get a job done. You know how to set priorities and accomplish them. You are a master of the "to do" list! Make it clear in the interview that you not only are willing to go the extra mile, but that you've had experience going several extra miles in your lifetime. For you, there is no mountain too high and no ocean too deep that it can't be conquered—and you've probably done a lot of conquering in your lifetime.

2. **Share your desire to learn.** You may have some extra miles on your personal "odometer," but that doesn't mean that you aren't excited about learning. As an older adult, you took the time to get your teacher certification, to further your education. Let an interviewer know that, for you, the learning doesn't stop because you have a degree or because you are of a certain age. If necessary, say to a principal, "I may not be up to speed on that issue right now, but I'm a learner and I'm willing to learn more!" Share your passion for continued learning at every possible opportunity.

FROM THE PRINCIPAL'S DESK:
"Nontraditional students should never say, 'I can't do that.' You would effectively 'shoot yourself in the foot' if you ever did."

3. **Demonstrate your time-management skills.** As a parent, or as an employee in the business world, you know how to manage time. You know how to organize, how to prioritize, and how to accomplish. You're a multi-tasker! As a classroom teacher, there are numerous tasks, chores, and assignments that must be handled on a daily basis. These may range from taking attendance to taking a lunch count, handling late-arriving students, and organizing instructional materials. It's important for you to share your (life) skills and (life) abilities in managing your time to accomplish several assignments—often at the same time.

4. **Showcase your discipline or behavior-management skills.** Kids talk out of turn, act up, misbehave, get into trouble, don't do what they're told, and so on. (You know the drill.) For more than 30 years, the general public has ranked classroom discipline at or near the top of their major concerns about American education. Principals, too, have concerns about classroom management and discipline. As you read the sample questions in this book, you know that you will be asked one or more questions about these issues. Count on it! This is a grand opportunity for you to show how your work record and/or role as a parent give you some unique experiences in behavior management. Make sure you come into an interview with a definite plan of action.

5. **Get up to speed on technology.** Just because you're older doesn't mean you shouldn't be aware of (and know how to use) the latest educational technology. Long before any interview, you need to take a course or several courses on educational technology, visit several schools to see what kinds of technology are being used in the classroom, talk with your younger classmates on the latest software being used, develop a network of friends and colleagues to share and discuss how technology is being used, and read the latest periodicals and magazines about technological issues facing classroom teachers. You can score some major points by demonstrating that your level of technological expertise is on a par with your younger classmates.

6. **Exude confidence.** Never think you are a "second-class" teacher because you're older than most of your classmates. Walk into an interview with your head held high, your feet firmly on the floor, and an attitude that says, "I'm just as good as (if not better than) any 22-year-old candidate!" This is not the time to play the shy, retiring individual. Show your confidence in every response to an interview question and in every experience you bring to the interview table. That confidence, in concert with your maturity, will convince any principal that you "have the goods" to be an excellent classroom teacher.

7. **Show your passion.** Let the interviewer know and feel your passion—for children, for teaching, for learning, and (most of all) for life.

8. **Demonstrate how your life skills transfer into the classroom.** You've traveled to a foreign country; show how that experience will help you be a better teacher of social studies. You've managed a family budget; show how that will help you teach practical applications of the math curriculum. You've cooked countless dinners; show how that will transfer to the science program and the promotion of inquiry-based science. You've tended to all manner of family illnesses, diseases, and sicknesses; show how that experience results in a thorough understanding of health. You've written diary entries, notes to school, and letters to friends; show how that relates to good communication and language arts skills. You are a voracious reader of both fiction and non-fiction; show how that will help you promote reading as a lifelong experience for students.

✔EXTRA CREDIT

Here's the key: Look at the elementary or secondary curriculum, and make matches between the subject matter and the wide array of life experiences you've had. Be sure to share those matches in the interview.

---

9. **Highlight your maturity.** While it is illegal for an interviewer to ask about your age, you should share several examples of how your maturity will be an asset to your success as a classroom teacher:

   • "Having raised three children to school age, I am keenly aware of how much psychology plays in the intellectual growth and development of youngsters."

   • "I was the executive secretary at a large business for 14 years. I have a good grasp of time management and can prioritize my work load with considerable ease."

   • "As the leader of a Sunday School class for the past eight years, I know how to motivate children through a 'hands-on, minds-on' curriculum."

   • "My volunteer work at the Salvation Army over the past decade has prepared me to deal with all kinds of people from all kinds of social situations."

   Your maturity (okay, your age) is a definite "positive." Demonstrate how all that experience will transfer into an elementary or secondary classroom, and you will literally soar above the competition.

10. **Be current.** Stay up to date on all the latest educational theories, practices, and issues. Know as much (if not more) than your younger classmates on the educational topics of the day. Try these helpful ideas:

- Access the Internet to learn what teachers are talking about, what concerns they have about teaching, and how they are solving their issues and problems.

- Join a listserv or a blog, and engage in an active dialogue with other teachers around the country.

- Read every educational periodical you can get your hands on, and discover what is going on locally, regionally, and nationally regarding education.

- Attend as many local or regional education conferences as you can, watch which sessions have the highest attendance, and find out more about those topics.

- Form an ad hoc group of other nontraditional students to explore various educational concerns and share them in a monthly meeting, group newsletter, or blog.

- Informally interview several principals (how about the principal at your child's school?) to learn about some of their concerns and challenges.

The Bottom Line

Here's the bottom line: There is often a misperception that because you are older you are not current. You can effectively crush that stereotype by demonstrating that you are just as current as—if not more than—any other college graduate by doing your educational homework well in advance of any interview. Knock the socks off the interviewer (figuratively speaking, of course) with both your breadth and depth of knowledge about any and all matters educational.

FROM THE PRINCIPAL'S DESK:

"For me, nontraditional teachers are in high demand. That's because they bring a passion for continued learning, a sincere dedication to teaching, and well-honed time-management skills. In addition, they are good team players, they are not afraid to branch out, and they are always willing to go the distance."

Your Personal Checklist for Interview Success

Before the Interview

- ☐ I know my strengths.
- ☐ I can translate my strengths into the needs of the school or district.
- ☐ All my communications are school-centered rather than self-centered.
- ☐ I can support my accomplishments with specific examples, anecdotes, or stories illustrating what I have done.
- ☐ I have gathered information about the school/district.
- ☐ I have prepared for any and all questions.
- ☐ I know how to respond if asked an illegal question.
- ☐ I have practiced questions with a friend or interested adult.
- ☐ I know about different interview types and settings.
- ☐ I know how to effectively communicate verbally.
- ☐ I know how I communicate nonverbally.
- ☐ I am aware of how to dress for success.
- ☐ I will arrive on time.

☐ I will treat everyone I meet as important.

☐ I will leave my cell phone in the car. Repeat: *I will leave my cell phone in the car.*

During the Interview

☐ I will greet the interviewer properly.

☐ I know how to use appropriate body language.

☐ I am prepared to respond to initial small talk in an interesting and positive manner.

☐ I can answer questions with complete sentences and with substance.

☐ I will keep the focus on the interviewer's needs.

☐ I will focus on exchanging useful information rather than on just getting the job.

☐ I will always emphasize the positive.

☐ I am able to turn any of my negatives into positives.

☐ I know how to engage in positive nonverbal cues.

☐ I have several questions to ask.

After the Interview

☐ I will record information about the interview before I leave the parking lot.

☐ I will ask myself questions about the interview.

☐ I will send a thank-you letter. Repeat: *I will send a thank-you letter.*

☐ I will immediately begin preparations for the next interview.

INDEX